AF440984

"TRAP BIBLE"

By Miguel Flores

2018

"Trap Bible"
Written by Miguel Flores
Illustrated by Along The Line @along.the.line

Standard Copyrights 2019 by Miguel Flores
Printed Autratrükk · www.aura.ee

Published by Miguel Flores
@miguelfloresIG

ISBN 978-9949-88-922-8 (Print)
ISBN 978-9949-88-923-5 (Kindle)

DISCLAIMER

INTRODUCTION

I stuffed my backpack between my legs, shoved the change in my pocket with the small piece of receipt paper and adjusted my body into a comfortable position on the seat. My mind was wandering through different scenarios of how the next hours will go and occasionally jumped back into episodes which happened during the day. I was glad, that the day had gone well. It was a special day, that was about to transform into an even more eventful night. There was excitement mixed with a pinch of fear deep in my stomach. It was subtle. So subtle that I could really notice it, only when I focused completely. I looked to my right and saw Mick's happy face that greeted me. He was emitting similar excitement to mine, but still it wasn't the same. For him, the night was about to be special in a different way, yet neither of them was more important than the other.

The sun was about to set and we were about a half an hour away from our destination. We sat in the bus, looked out of the windows following whatever glimpsed before our eyes, occasionally engaging in small talk. Before we passed the half-way mark on our road, Mick pulled out a small piece of paper which reminded me of a chopped up postmark. He carefully ripped it in half, handing me a piece while instructing me to put it under my tongue. I didn't know if I was supposed to chew on it for a bit and spit it out or if I was supposed to swallow it, so I asked. I don't remember, what Mick told me, but it didn't resonate with me in a negative way, so I accepted it and did what I was told.

The bus reached its final destination. Right side of the bus sank a couple degrees, as it made a different engine noise, which indicated that it was time for us to exit. We picked up our bags and left the bus. As soon as we stepped on the pavement, fresh air and wild wind hit my face. I could feel the worries and bothers associated with the city being washed away, as the air filled my lungs with energy. The sun was setting behind a freshly gathered field. All different shades of orange, red and golden filled the sky adding completely new dimensions and effects to the few clouds that floated in the golden sky. We looked at the road, field and the forest at the border of which we were standing. Everything looked as if it had not only a visual filter over it, but also an emotional one, that was turning every sensation into a positive and amplified it to new levels. That buzz and slight discomfort, that I felt on my skin after I took that piece of paper started to wear off, returning me to the pleasant state of being. We had about a kilometre to walk. Half of it was going through a small living area that was built in soviet times as a getaway for people who had good jobs, that was now either an old summer house or an updated home for an upper middle class family. The second half of the road went right through the woods, sided by pines and a peacefully flowing river. The air in the area was cooler than in the city. It was especially well defined on the border of the woods, where the road entered the thick forest.
Once again I set my foot on the broken rocky road that I've walked countless times during so many events that I could write a book about it. Small stones cracked under my feet. I was making my way deeper into the woods. Sounds of birds singing, wind rushing the top of trees and branches crackling became louder and louder, pushing out all industrial buzzing and unnaturally sharp noises. Slowly transmuting the ambience into being, that is much more in tune with itself and everything surrounding it. After 13 years of walking that road, I've managed to memorise many trees, stumps, holes and ant houses. Yet this time I could notice much more detail and something else was different too. I saw everything in a new,

more saturated light. Everything was sharper and it felt, as if all that was surrounding me was breathing, though very subtly. I shared my notes with Mick, which he quickly evaluated and confirmed. Then I noticed how behind the trees and bushes, I could see outlines of a building. The road changed from a rocky, broken up countryside road to a stone one. Seconds later, a yellow house became visible. We had arrived to our first destination. We were feeling great and ready to embrace whatever was about to come. In a split second, thousands of memories had strobed in front of my eyes and a warm feeling of being in a beloved place came over me. I knew that everything that was going to happen that night, was going to change my life for the better. Better, at the time, was exactly what my unhealthy confused mind needed. Since after years of depression I didn't feel like I had much to lose.
I stumbled around the yard for a bit before I entered the house, still taking in the experience of returning to the location where my childhood took place.
The house radiated warmth and peace. Dimmed lighting and classic music made the whole atmosphere even more loving and welcoming. My younger brother was home too, even though he didn't come out of his room. We didn't interact with him much, other than the exchange of some small words while he was on his way to get some food.
I went up to the second floor to leave my bags and excess clothes in the guest's room in which I stay when I come around as my old bedroom was rebuilt into a meditation room/ wardrobe. On my way up the stairs there was a lamp that was illuminating the staircase. For my whole life, I've remembered it to have a very bright, yellowish white hue, but this time it was a gloomy pine green. As soon as I noticed it I stopped and stared at it for a while. I was trying to understand, how did it turn to green? Or was it one of the effects? After a bit of observation, I noticed that it indeed was green in my perspective, as the whole staircase and the walls were green. I also noticed, that staring at the bright light didn't hurt my eyes at all. After about two minutes of looking and evaluating, I let

go of the lamp and continued my way to the guest's bedroom. It was right by the staircase on my right. I opened the squeaky door and dropped my bags on the floor, turned around and went back the hall. The curiosity in me started to grow and a great yet peaceful feeling washed over me and sucked out all the worry that was weighing on my shoulders and in my being.

I walked around the house and went to all the rooms that I had walked through for years, as I observed the changes I could perceive with my vision. The most significant change that I had noticed was that lights had changed the colour of their hue. Upon deeper observation, I started to notice small patterns occur on the surface of the objects that I had stared at. Everything seemed to be more alive. The house was no longer just a house. Not just stone walls and furniture and lights, but it was all alive. The house was a separate yet universally unified being. It had its own breath and lived its own life. It felt with us and lived along to our story, slightly holding it and transforming itself along the infinite escalation of time and our lives and actions. The rooms had their own spirits, every room spoke about its purpose and how the purpose was fulfilled in it. Each painting on the wall had its own story that it transmitted constantly. Everything that was there and wasn't there visibly made more sense and quietly spoke without words that my ears could hear, yet my heart could feel.

Mick was minding his own business, he was on the third floor, possibly meditating or going through his lyrics written on countless pages of A4 that he keeps folded in his bag.

That evening time didn't matter, the clock on my phone's screen and the ticking machines on walls didn't matter. The concept of time itself lost any meaning or value. I was in the eternal moment that is now. I didn't have any past and my future was composed before my eyes by my internal processes, thoughts and actions. I didn't have anything that my mind would say it *"has"* to do, nor did I have any obligations. I simply was. The voice in my head that's usually loud and incoherent at most, was quiet. Because it was unable to compose any sensible sentences. My being was only influenced by the images and senses that arose inside of me. In that moment, all of them were peaceful and pleasant.

Though the concept nor my perception of time didn't matter I could still understand that it was no longer sunset outside and that the sky was now pitch black, with some glimpses of yellowish blue that hued from the sun floating far behind the horizon. I went upstairs, passing the green lights up until the moment when my eyes could see Mick.

He was sitting on a mattress, doing exactly what I thought he was doing. Acknowledging that pleased the mind, but to my awareness. It wasn't hot nor cold thus I offered to go outside, because in that moment I felt the desire to leave the house and explore, in order to see what the universe has to offer. He stood up quickly with a smile on his face and we shuffled down the stairs to the ground floor. Within my sub consciousness I knew, that it was summer, so there was no need to put on any extra layers. Then, something told me that I should go out barefoot. I obeyed the suggestion and as I opened the door the now natural warmth of the house was met with a cooler flow of air. As my body reacted to it I felt that it was cold, but not too cold to turn around and put on a jacket. The cold that went up my naked feet as they contacted the stone, was much more detailed than ever before. It felt like every nerve, that was on the bottom of my foot was reacting exponentially quicker and somehow thus more stimulated to give more responses than usual. In a way I could say, that it felt as if small needles of cold were poking at my feet with every step made. But the so called poking wasn't painful. It resembled a sensation of soft electricity being struck into my feet. My lungs filled with fresh night air and the energy that came with it filled my whole being. As I set my foot on the grass. The nerves within my feet exploded with sensation. It was so casual and yet completely new. I felt the cold on my feet and the air in my lungs, and with that feeling, came deep understanding of the moment and the gratitude for existence and simple being arose deep within me. I was glad to be there,

I was glad to be alive. It didn't matter what I had done or how events had turned out or made me feel. None of my past conflicts and misunderstandings mattered. All that had any value to it was the moment.

As all my past, all my evaluations of past experiences and expectations were stripped away. I was once again amazed by what I saw. Maybe it wasn't that I was amazed by what I saw, but more astonished by being able to see it in a new light. A light, that wasn't modified or corrupted by filters, which were put over my eyes by my parents, teachers, friends and media.

I looked up into the sky and I saw stars. Hundreds of thousands of stars. They were much brighter than ever before. I don't know if my vision was much clearer and sharper, or on that special day the light pollution was minimal for some reason. The same sky, that I had looked at every night of my life, was completely new. I saw the same old stars and satellites that I've seen my whole life. The same stars my parents and their parents had looked at. Yet that night, all the stars were shining. I could see the milky way and how there were clusters of stars here and there. Blinking didn't strip the beauty away from my eyes. It wasn't a dream or a hallucination, I was awake and I was more awake than I had ever been before in my life. The breathtaking moment was a million times more exciting than watching any Ultra HD TV or watching a movie about space. It was not the same, as the picture that I once observed with my eyes on a screen was now right there. There were no, so to say middlemen. I was the camera, I had the best lenses and the picture I was watching was alive and right there in front of me, yet a million light years away.

As I was looking up into the sky, I made my feet comfortable with the cold ground I was standing on and something had sucked my awareness out of my body.

I was sucked into my past. I can't clearly remember into which of my experiences I was going through, but all I can say is that those events were the ones, that had caused me the most pain and discomfort in my life. Something had walked me through my whole life, every experience that I didn't understand, every moment that was misunderstood by me and every situation in which I got hurt or ones that left me scarred. I was an observer, the third person. I was silent and observed how those events were escalating. I saw what happened with a new much more advanced, yet neutral perspective. I could now understand, why one or the other event had happened and what the lesson behind it was. In each event that I was observing, I could now see love and reason. I could see the purpose behind it and seeing all those things brought me to the place of deep appreciation. With that, my mind started to crack its walls. It had built for protecting its fragile understanding of life, that was surrounded by sadness and misunderstanding. All that was once filtering all the input and output was now put aside and I could see and evaluate everything much clearer. The inner voice, that was once blaming me for everything, talking me down and narrating negative scenarios, was now quiet. I could see myself in a completely new light, without any blame. I also remembered all four years of deep depression that I went through. I remembered and saw clearly every moment that I had taken in a twisted way, simply because the depressed outlook on life and my conditioned mind told me to do so. All the unnecessary self-inflicted suffering that I had put myself through was now visible. I could also clearly make out when and how my mind was talking to me in a belittling way and made me feel worse, than I should.

Looking at the stars, it all made sense. As it made sense it no longer mattered nor had any value. The continuous moment I was looking at the stars, I consciously made peace with all my past, every moment and event. I made peace with the depression and happily let it go, as I no longer needed it. That night, I fell in love with my story. It made sense. Everything that

I had gone through had brought me to that very moment and that moment was there to be a landmark on my path. I felt a great feeling of gratitude, as everything that had happened has shaped me into the person that I am now and had taught me a valuable lesson that made me stronger and smarter, as well as it gave me the ability to be more practical and perform better. At that moment I remembered how beautiful life was and the colours that once lost their saturation, had filled with intensity and radiated the energy of life, that I once let flow right past me. The same second as all the weight of my past had fallen off my shoulders, I felt relieved and the energy that filled my body brought back my desire to live and express. That late summer night, I saw the light at the end of the tunnel. I felt its calling and I started crawling towards it, even though surrounded by mysterious blackness and the infinite unknown that was now before me to explore. The loving call of my true self was too sweet to resist, so I followed.

BIRTH OF THIS BOOK

When I started writing this book, I wrote it in diary/ memoire form. The purpose of it was pretty simple. To deconstruct some elements of my life in order to improve it and have a record of some events, thoughts and ideas. As much as I can remember, why I even began writing on paper in the first place was because I always enjoyed putting effort into my handwriting and as I got older, the process of writing became relaxing, like a recorded meditation that I can go over later if I want to.

Throughout my youth I've had many diaries and notebooks. I've always loved writing small notes and making up To-Do lists to be more productive and organised. Some periods I wrote more and some periods I barely picked up the pen. Yet the older I got and more books I've gone through, the more I started to value writing and the profound effects it can bring if used properly. In that escalating time or event, however you want to call it, I started writing on a daily basis and dedicating amounts of time to it. All of a sudden, every day I found myself waking up eager to experience new things so later I could sit somewhere in a nice ambient place, drink some hot beverage and deconstruct and illustrate what has happened to me during that day or some days prior. I started to spend time choosing pens and ink that work the best for me and flow the smoothest. With that came along understanding of paper and how different papers manufactures had a different feel to them and how some pens worked with some papers and how others didn't do as good. It almost became a routine to go to bookstores to buy new books to read, so I could expand my perspective and choosing new empty diary books by their covers. With time, as the same diary books were stacked into piles and pages on pages were filled with ink, I get fond of joking about me later spending weeks to months on rewriting those handwritten entries and stories into digital documents and then polishing them and compiling into chapters. At some point even, I joked about it so much it started to get to me and I had to spend some time looking for software that could scan my handwriting and paste it into a document. Gladly I found it and was relieved by the fact that the better the handwriting, the easier it will be for the software to scan it and write it properly.

As I mentioned before, at first I didn't plan to write a book and whatever will be written later was simply meant to be my own studies on life and universe around me and nothing more. Ironically enough, every major thing in my life started from something that wasn't that serious.

Though when I felt the desire to compile my studies and so to say *"knowledge"* into a book, I started to put more effort into making it as understandable, simple and practical as possible. At some point in the beginning of this process, I thought to myself: *"Will I be able to write enough pages of interesting and valid content, that I would even be able to put a book together?"*, but when I was around a physical page number 1000, I quickly understood, that I might need to make multiple books, as releasing a tomb of over a thousand pages might leave an impression that I wrote a new bible and am trying to start some shit.

Before getting into the book and its contents, if you didn't already skip the introduction. I would like to clarify something that has been ringing in my head ever since I decided that one day this book or books will be released. As I've red many books that can be labeled as similar to mine or can be simply put in the same genre or category, I think what I'm about to say is rather important and should be considered while reading this book. The purpose of this book is entertainment. For me it was entertaining to be in the process of writing it. It was entertaining to talk to people about the book or to meet people who came along in the process or as a result of me writing it. For whoever is reading it, foremost the book is meant to be enjoyed as an entertaining piece of literature. If you're enjoying reading it, then it's doing its purpose. If you happen to find something in the book, that answers some of your questions, helps you to get through something or makes your life better in any way. Even better.

However, if you didn't enjoy the book, think that it's completely invalid, that it's fiction or a monologue of a psychopath and decide to quit reading it. So be it. Guess it wasn't meant for you.

Why I included the disclaimer was because again, I've red many books that are about someone experiencing something or someone explaining something about this collective universe we're living in. Many books that were teaching this and that and how to be or do things that seem impossible at first. One common thing that I noticed in many of those books that made me not trust the author that much, was the fact that oddly enough many of them talked in a manner in which some believed to be a sort of advanced teacher and guru. That they were superior to many and that one had to follow every word they said in order to reach the same level of spiritual or financial wellbeing that they had. Many of them were talking about essentially true things and practices that are real, but again, in such old and misleading ways that it may often misguide people into hurting themselves more than helping.

To explain myself a bit better and not to sound like I'm discrediting many authors in the intro of my first book. You've probably heard or read a couple of stories or articles or maybe even red a whole book about meditations and yoga. Some say, that if you meditate for 8 hours a day, move to mountains, stop eating any meat and give up all the pleasures of life. You will achieve some magical state of awareness and being where you will be one with the universe or god and you will know infinite love. Sounds amazing right? I'm not saying that it's impossible or not worth it, but think about it. If you do all that and will get to that point. What's the point of having a physical body or even being born into this world? Were we born into bodies and into this society, to let go of it? Or were we born to learn, explore, experience, love and create in harmony with this world and each other? I think the last one sounds a bit better. So many of those authors and books speak of things that are essentially true, but if approached internally and not evaluated from many angles, they may bring more harm than harmony for some people. I've personally learned, that it's much better to take from those books, what can be used in my day to day life, so I could better it and live in a more balanced and happy way.

The thing about the authors, which I had mentioned above, is that many of those authors portray themselves as very advanced spiritual or financial individuals (depends on what type of books you read) who have achieved a lot and who are so good at what they're doing, that people start to follow them blindly and do everything they say. Those authors position themselves as gurus, who start to build small, pretty harmless but still, cult type things. When you really start to look into those people. Who are they behind their books, and what goes on in their current lives? You can see many things that are first, out of balance with the contents of their books and second, in many areas you don't really want to live or be like them. So why would you follow a person who is not an example of what you want to achieve? Would you take advice on how to be happy from a deeply depressed person? Not really.

So in case if anything in the text above is still unclear. I'm not discrediting the authors. All I'm saying is, that everything should be taken with a bit of healthy skepticism and a grain of salt. And that if someone wants to use someone else to better their life, it's better to be very aware of why you want to learn from a specific person and if they really are an example of what you're trying to reach or is it just an image.

In my book, I try not to sound like a teacher and I don't want to put myself above or below anyone. If anything, I'd describe myself as a stepping stone. If you are looking for answers or for help in this book. Don't take everything literally. Read it and evaluate it. And should you feel like I'm describing an example or am being an example of what you're trying to be in your own way, take it as another hint from the universe or god and try to implement it in your life. If it does stick and help, great.
If not, simply move on and don't stress yourself over it. After all, this book is meant to entertain you.
I hope you enjoy what you're about to read.

ABOUT THIS BODY

I've always had big dreams and goals that I was eager to achieve. Ever since I can remember, my imagination was always busy running through different scenarios of how my life could go. If you have watched the movie *"Mr. Nobody"*, then my imagination was similar to what was going on in the movie. As far as my memory stretches, I've always seen life and this world as something beautiful and fascinating, somewhat magical (even though I don't like the word magic). Since I learned how to speak, I started bombarding my parents and grandparents with questions about the place I was born into. Why are things the way they are? How does this work? What happens if I do this or that?

I remember my grandmother once told me, that when I was a kid, I used to ask so many questions and new questions from previous ones, that she got tired of answering them and simply told me that she didn't know. From my mother's side too, I've heard throughout my childhood, that I was a very adventurous and curious child. In some cases my parents told me not to ask *"stupid questions"*, even though I quickly figured out, the questions I was asking weren't stupid. The answers either didn't matter or my parents simply didn't know an answer that would tell me something. That never stopped me though. I continued asking the questions. Went out there to test ideas on myself or asked somebody else, until I got the answer or forgot the question.

Turning into my teens, something happened what often is common with other teenagers. I turned reckless, ignorant and on my way to exploring new things and roads. Roads that weren't healthy for me in any way nor the relationships I had at the time. I went through several years of deep depression and other unpleasant things I might talk about later on, if they seem useful to talk about.

During my teenage years and those years filled with depression, I did dream, work and grow onto my true path too, though without awareness. For that I'm extremely happy and grateful. Yet if I put myself back into those times, I'd say it's not pleasant being there and I'd much rather erase those things from my history. Yet, looking at it in a retrospective, I'm very much pleased, that those things happened to me the way they did and that I had to go through them, because those were the events that taught me valuable lessons and shaped me into the person I am now. So in that relatively small period of time, my curiosity and excitement about life were pretty low, as well as my ability to be aware in the moment. Yet, it all got better. Curiosity returned and depression faded. With that, energy, awareness and the desire to explore life returned and from then on I started reevaluating my dreams and life again.

When I got out of depression, I developed a huge fascination over this world. Over how it worked and how I could be a harmonious piece of this world and work with it together in peace. From there on, I started on a daily basis to work on myself in every way I could. I started studying my experiences and reading new books to see, what other people had experienced. As it seems to me now, when I started walking my true path with awareness, the same *Universe** started giving me signs and profound experiences through people who were put on my path. Not to make it all sound so flowery and nice. Some people were very unpleasant and some experiences were dangerous to say the least.

Yet, looking back at any experience, it happened for a reason and taught a valuable lesson. What I also learned later, was that if I learned to enjoy any experience and acknowledge later, then soon I will be grateful for it. Experiencing things and difficult situations becomes much easier and even pleasant in the long way.

Universe - We're all familiar with this term and how it can be used. To be as clear in my texts as possible. I would like to clarify, that here, the universe is the whole space we're in with all the things that we see and don't see. In case if it's written with a capital letter that I hopefully remembered to capitalise, I mean it in a sense of god like awareness that is everywhere and that is in every one of us. So for example: I'm curious about how the universe works. While I was figuring that, I also learned that I was the Universe I was curious about and that I am learning my own inner, deeper self.

Side note: As I started using diaries as tools and ways to work with myself. Deconstructing myself and all planes of me, as well as deconstructing the world I'm living in, became a very big part of my life as well as a very powerful tool of improving my life. I started to pay attention to what goes on around me and inside of me, how one or the other affected the opposite and what type of united result it brought out. The pages of my diaries turned into research about self and about the mysterious surrounding world. The more I started to get into the depths of my world, more vast grounds I started to explore. And how written deconstructing became my primary tool of evaluating what was going on in that seemingly new world.

DECONSTRUCTING

One additional minor disclaimer I'd like to add is that in this book, some terms and their meanings are not the same as in dictionaries and on the world web. They are similar and come from the same place, but some details differ. To understand the book at its best. I advise to read it with an open mind.

For me, deconstructing is an ongoing process where all elements may change and different meanings and lessons may emerge in the process and with time. Deconstructing is a process that can be applied to events and things in the past, as well as the events which are unfolding as you're experiencing them in the moment. As the universe, mind and everything around us essentially is infinite, so is the process of deconstructing, as more you pursue it, more your awareness will grow and more new perspectives you'll be able to adopt. Simply put. Deconstructing is a process of picking something apart *(de-constructing)*. In this case, we can pick anything apart with our mind, heart and awareness. That gives us the ability to adopt new perspectives, thus see things from new angles. To pragmatically switch between those angles and gives us the ability to choose the most effective methods to use in the given situation. I think that all of us at some point in our lives, have felt as if life was chaotic and nothing made sense. I haven't lived a life of someone else, so I can't speak for other people, but personally I can confirm, that at least in the past I've had many of those moments and back then I didn't know how to approach them. Discovering "deconstructing" was something that made my life much easier.

Despite it sounding like a TopShop infomercial, I wouldn't spend my time writing about this thing and using it in my everyday life, if it wasn't something worthy sharing. Especially when I'm definitely not the first one to write about it as I've seen it in a few books myself. So in a practical way. Deconstructing is a practice/method/tool for arranging chaotic events into order and being able to understand the purpose behind some things and how everything is in universal balance and how you're an equal part of it, as well as the whole thing at the same time.

Deconstructing can be applied to simple and complex things, as well as seemingly chaotic or supernatural. Some take a little energy and some take days or years to figure out. Some are like life, prolonged process that may not even have an end. Sometimes deconstructing will bring you to a deep understanding of some subject or will give you some practice that you can use to achieve something more effectively and in a more personalised way. In other cases, deconstructing will spawn more questions and at first, seemingly create even more confusion. Yet, if it's approached with an optimistic attitude and an open mind. - The fog will disappear quickly and new answers will emerge as if out of nowhere.

While writing and rewriting this book, as I'm reading over the paragraphs I think to myself. Does it make sense to someone who doesn't think in a similar way or hasn't read the books that had influenced my way of thinking? Because I want to keep the book as raw and close to earth as possible, I don't want to edit it too much and go over each entry overwriting it and rearranging the whole thing. Not to discourage, if some things don't make sense at first. You will understand them along the way as I'll start explaining them later on as well as some answers will come out in my deconstruction diaries, plus you might start noticing those things in your own life as well (if that happens, you will just know). Like with many books, this one might also need to be read multiple times. If it's interesting enough of course. Another thing that is worthy of mentioning.

There are also some questions that are of a more complex nature. For example paradoxes. For example, where the start of the universe is or what is the purpose of it. You can answer them to an extent with your mind and the words we use to communicate, but if you try to explain them in a deeper way using only words and understandings, which we have adopted in our current society. You might waste a grand amount of your energy and time into nothingness and end up with no substantial answer that would satisfy you or with even more questions and confusion. These questions don't really need answering. It's like an argument between two people who have never been to space or have no way of going there, if the Earth is flat or global. Be it one or the other, it would be cool to know, but the knowledge itself is not useful for neither of those people. With time, you'll understand why.

In this book, you may encounter me using the "Flat Earth Global Earth" example quite a lot. Not because I have anything against people who believe in Flat Earth or that I'm trying to poke fun at them. It's just that personally, I feel like this example is a simple way to illustrate that firstly we should handle the questions that are present and affect our lives and then the ones that seem interesting, but don't really affect us in any way.

To be even more clear. Imagine as if you and I are arguing about our Earth being flat or a globe. I can be on any side of this argument and so can you. If you feel like putting me into the position of a flat earther, then so be it.
We can talk endlessly about our theories, conspiracies and things we consider facts and bring out whatever scientists or anyone whose opinion we respect have said. But now let's step away from ourselves and look at the situation from a third person's perspective and let's lift that perspective higher.
Does it really matter if the Earth is flat or not? How would your life change or how would that knowledge affect your life? Would you wake up earlier or all of a sudden start eating healthy? If tomorrow it got confirmed, that the Earth was flat. Would you get paid more or live a happier life? Or if it got confirmed that the Earth is a massive

globe, that floats in the blackness of space. Would that solve any real and serious world conflicts or issues?

If you mind your own business you'll have more energy, less chaos, and less confusion. The less senseless questions and you'll spend your time in a much more mindful way, than you could ever imagine.
Ask questions about things that really matter to you. Deconstruct situations that are happening in your life or happened to others, but may also have effects on yours.
Don't fill your head with things that suck out your energy and create more confusion. Just to create an illusion of being productive in the process of deconstructing.

PRACTICAL DECONSTRUCTING

Imagine this situation. You're home. You're in a good mood and you decide to invite a friend over because you haven't seen them in a long time. You call them up, they reply and head out. On the phone, the conversation was cheerful on both sides. You're preparing your home and yourself to see your friend. You're ready to have a nice conversation with them and spend some good time together.
The friend arrives and as he/she walks in, you can clearly see, that something about them is not quite right. They're not as happy as they sounded on the phone and you can see from their facial expression, that something's on their mind. You can ask if something's wrong, but in this case, you are told that everything's fine. You dismiss that thought and start chatting.
You're telling your stories with great excitement, with emotion and taking it into the details.
Then you start to notice again, that something's not right. They're not really paying attention to what you're saying. Now at this point you may be getting irritated or disappointed, depending on how you usually react. Let's imagine that in this case you're a patient, so you decide to ask them about how are they're doing. Their side of the story is not so exciting. They quickly go over their recent past aka a lot of work because they need to pay their bills or whatever. When you ask them a question about anything, you get an irritated, quick response as if they were throwing some half ass answers at you. At this point you're no longer enjoying the conversation and ask them again, if something is wrong and again, you get

an annoyed response. Something similar to *"None of your business"* and then they decide to leave.

Now he/she's leaving your home while leaving you out of balance and without the happiness with which you welcomed them into your home. They don't give you any explanations and simply leave on an unrestful note. I think some of us have been in a similar situation. The one that I described above is a very primitive and childlike example, because I wanted to be as simple as possible, so the example of deconstructing it wouldn't take another chapter. As many people as there are, so many responses there are for these situations. Some get sad, and some get extremely angry or anxious. Emotional responses are different and so are the physical responses that follow. Some may only experience increase in their heart rate, some can be brought as far as fainting.

This can be the first place where you start to use deconstructing as a practice and a method to better your everyday life. In this case. In the process of deconstructing, you get to see the situation again and again from many different angles. You get to experience it over and over again, but without the same emotional attachment, which will allow you to see the situation in the new light and notice details that you never considered before.

Let's start with the friend being all positive on the phone and arriving in a distraught state of being. Maybe they remembered something that bothered them for a long time and couldn't get it off their mind? Maybe on their way to your home, they received a phone call from their boss, who told them that they were about to be fired? There are infinite situations that could have happened to the person on their way to your house, which might have influenced their being upon arrival.
Next thing is that even though they didn't pay attention much, they still listened to you and spend time with you, until it went downhill from there. Were the things that you told them that

important in which they had to listen to you with their full attention? Or were you just sharing your experiences for the sake of conversation or showing them, that you were doing well? Again, the possibilities are infinite and chances are, that the things you were telling them were not that important to be bothered by them not paying full attention.

Then, even though they brought a bad vibe with them. Did you really have to take it personally? Did it really have to bother you, or you chose to be bothered out of habit or because of your ego? The more you think about it, the more you start to understand, that whatever happened is not that serious and is not really worth feeling bad about. Again, however they were feeling or whatever was bothering them in their life and in their world. It is not present in your world and you should not keep the weight of it on you after the person has left. Even in their presence, you don't have to carry their weight. You can simply listen to them and be compassionate and if you have good advice which could actually help. You may offer it to them.

If you learn to deconstruct things like that in an effective way. You will also learn to let go of unhealthy emotional habits and rewire your brain to adopt a new healthier pattern of living.

From that, for example. If in the past you were irritated by something you didn't understand or it just happened. After deconstructing and putting in some effort into applying the new knowledge to your lifestyle. You'll notice, that thing no longer irritates you. You'll notice that it is still there, you'll acknowledge that you used to be bothered by it. But the deeper your understanding of the more you'll be in peace with it as you now know, why it is the way it is.

So that was a small example of how deconstructing works in my understanding of it and how it can be applied to life in a simple and quick, yet practical way to better one's life.

CHAPTER I:
THE FIRST MORNING

I opened my eyes quickly, not like in the movies where people open their eyes slowly or where the camera slowly fades from black into the view of the bedroom. The first thing I noticed was the soft light that was shining into the bedroom. Then I noticed the peaceful and rested feeling that was present in my being and how my inner voice was much more peaceful. It didn't start to think about all the possible negative scenarios that could or could not come to life.
I remembered what had happened last night and decided to go over it one more time in my head, to hopefully confirm the positive changes that went down a couple hours prior. Just as I was hoping, everything that stars had showed me was true and now took valid place in my existence.
Despite being able to feel happiness again and knowing, that everything was going to be alright, I knew, that still if I wanted to achieve my goals and get to the balanced being, that the night had shown me. I had a lot of learning and self-discovery to achieve. I had countless days and nights of redefining my understanding of self to come. I wasn't just on my way to recovery and discovery of my personal story. I was only becoming aware of me having feet and that they can be used for walking. There was a vast unexplored world of potential and opportunities before me which somewhere had something that was calling me. I could indeed feel the calling now, but to get to it, I had to learn how to walk. I had a long road to walk and I also had to learn how to manage my energy and how to

interact with my surrounding in a new way, to actually get where I want to be.

A sting hit my stomach, telling me that I was hungry. I threw the blanket off of my naked body and the cool breeze washed my body with uncomfortable chill, quickly waking me up to reality. I pulled on a shirt and pants as quickly as I possibly could, to avoid that cold feeling and walked out of the room.
It was bright outside. The sun was shining and there were only few white clouds floating in the sky. I didn't know what time it was and to be honest, it still didn't matter. I didn't waste my attention on looking for clocks. Everybody else was still sleeping. Mick, as well as my brother were sleeping in their rooms. I could hear both of them snore. Arriving in the kitchen, I opened the fridge and grabbed whatever I considered breakfast. As my mother has been avoiding meats and all sorts of modified and processed foods, the fridge wasn't exactly very versatile with its contents. I took whatever I could make a cereal bowl from. The feeling that was left in me after the night was interesting. Everything was no longer breathing and the colours of lamps turned back to normal, yet everything maintained the aspect of being alive.

The first thing I learned that day, was that not being depressed was amazing. The new type of excitement that was in me motivated me to do things with more dedication and more passion. To try new things and find out more about the world, that was surrounding me. I understood, that depression put a negative filter over my life and programmed my inner voice to sabotage my inner being by making me feel worthless. As the understanding was sinking in my guts, I started to feel the need to change many aspects of my life. I had to apply changes to my mind and to the way I was thinking. To the way I reacted to things and how I treated people. In general, I started to see how everything is connected in one way or the other and that if I wanted to live a better life, I had to change myself first, before I could change anything else. Though I was motivated, I didn't rush into changing myself. I decided, that it was a much better idea, to start making lists of things that I wanted to improve and start working on them, as it's easier to follow a plan, rather than continue running around incoherently trying to get something done.

Side note: I'll let the new information sink in my consciousness, slowly letting every small fraction of an experience fall on its shelf in my mind. With time, I started to adopt the peaceful way of communicating with my inner voice and whatever happened that night, started to make sense.
I started to notice, how what I experienced then had influenced my being later on and opened my mind to a whole world of new possibilities and simultaneously showed to me how all experience and knowledge can be applied for personal and common wellbeing and benefit.

As the time passed, memories and recollection of the night faded, and with them so did the importance of that night. It became just another night in my life that had any significance only when I was grateful for the progress that has been made. And when in some conversations the dialogue was about my story of escaping depression or individuals discussing their trips. Still, there are times when the night comes back to my mind and I re-experience it to its full extent, as if a part of my consciousness was returning to the night to enjoy its peace and beauty. Emotionally its a pleasant memory to keep. Its cozy and warm, it involves my favourite souls on this planet and being able to witness the Milky Way with my own eyes was simply mesmerising. But that's about it. Emotions don't heat the house and don't put food on your table, so I left it at that. I was more about the practical use of the knowledge, that was stuck into my head during that night and how could I apply it to my life to make it better and truly use the experience I was given for a profound purpose. Even if it was profound only to myself.

It took some time to pick the experience apart into small bits and look at them from different angles. The most unusual part was looking at the bits of the experience, as well as at the whole without any emotional attachments or filters, because those exact filters were stripped off of me by the experience. Therefore applying filters to observe something that is teaching me how to observe and work with things without filters would be corrupting the process. It took some time to learn how to let go of emotional attachments in a way that actually made me feel different. At first it was hard, but as I started to see, how it changed my state of being and how it helped me in many situations. My mind started to understand, that letting go of attachments to emotions, outcomes and expectations that made a big change in how I felt during different events. That not being attached eased my being and allowed me to apply many more solutions, to get to the outcomes I desired.
Being able to observe the experiences that I went through during that night without attaching myself to some emotion or idea made me see, that when I'm not attached to anything, I see the whole spectre of angles and ways on how I can approach the subject or object. Even better, it didn't make me feel any type of way while it gave me much more understanding than ever before.

Later on in this book, I will get into depth with explaining into what I believe emotional attachment to be and what I've noticed it affect in my life. To maintain some type of escalation in this book and try to maintain a sort of linear movement. Right now I will only say, that emotional attachment is us or in this case me choosing to bond myself with something through emotion. Choosing to feel worried about how will a job interview go, because I choose to think, that the given job is what I need and that there is no other way to get to where I want (because just getting a job can't be the final result one is striving for). So emotional attachment is choosing to feel some type of way towards something, because of whatever reason the mind and ego give.

To share some food for thoughts, I can offer a practice. Try imagining any or as many interactions you are a part of. Especially good are the ones where you think you play an important role. It can be you being a CEO of a company or you doing some task in a team. Now imagine that process going on but without you being involved. As if you never existed, you've never been there, you've never been any part of it. Of course it's a completely different universe, but you can clearly see all of those processes peacefully functioning without you. If for example you chose to be a CEO, imagine them having a different CEO and the company functions just as well without you being present. Often we may think that we are very important or that the task we are doing is of utmost value, but in reality. You just choose to feel that way. I'm not saying that it's bad, but often we let those attachments take control over us and make us feel stressed or too important in way too many real life examples. So I'm not saying, emotional attachment is bad, even if I happened to leave such an impression. All I'm saying is that it's good to monitor it and know where you're giving your energy away in an unnecessary manner.

The first big thing I started to take care of was my inner voice. The voice which was talking in my head and in my own voice. I think at least few readers could relate to having that voice in their heads. So it happens that the voice is pretty incoherent. Talks about anything and everything without pause, exhausting and taking focus away. During depression the voice was not friendly at all. Even though I thought it was my voice and I was guiding it. It was living a completely separate life. It had its own thoughts and fears and as it was living inside of my head, it was projecting its fears and thoughts on me and thus made me feel bad and deeply unhappy. The night I've been talking about so far made me see the voice in my head for what it really is.

In a sense I could call it the voice of my mind. During depression, it was abusive. That night, it wasn't abusive anymore. As it is understood, the depression was making the mind feel unpleasant too and that if we changed our ways of thinking and coexisting, we could get to better results and live a happier life.

Of course the understanding wasn't enough to bring a significant change. The understanding only brought the matter to awareness and now there was a long process of reconditioning the mind and unlearning old and adopting new habits. There started my journey on exploring the mind, reconditioning it to be in harmony with itself, myself and later on, to harmoniously experience and express to the whole vast reality in front of me.

INNER VOICE AS MIND

I already mentioned above, that the Inner Voice has a life of its own and it resides inside your head. It floats formlessly somewhere in the back of your skull, talking and projecting images in your head. It's been there for so long and it's been so comfortable and subtle, yet right in your face, that for your whole life, it has created an elaborate illusion of being the one. Often the inner voice is incoherent and can't stay on one subject for more than 10 seconds. It loves to worry and talk a lot about things that don't matter. Sometimes it does help with evaluating things and getting across obstacles in our physical world and solving problems regarding survival and achieving goals. Yet it has dominated a lot of people and taken control for itself. If I was to illustrate the subject, I'd describe it as a person having a pet, that is there to help them, but the pet decides to hypnotise the person and take control over them, while the person thinks that the will of the pet companion is the will of the person.

Even though the inner voice has had control over me for years, it has also brought a lot of joy and many accomplishments to me. When I started to get into what the inner voice is and how it affects me. I started to ask that question from myself, as well as started reading different books, that seemed to carry any answers. What I noticed in many books and heard from many people who had influence on many people through leading some movements or simply being influential writers, was that they all called the inner voice either the mind or the ego and both of them described it to be some sort of an alien force or an enemy. At the time, lack of personal knowledge and experience and in a way still being stuck in my old mindset. I didn't know any better, so I took into consideration what I heard and tried to extract the valuable essence out of it. Many books and so called teachers expressed, that in order to obtain peace and clarity and later on, oneness with the world. It was necessary to conquer the inner voice by constantly battling and suppressing it, as if it was some sort of a tyrant who resided in your head. All of them shared similar practices, exercises and meditations that were supposed to help. Even though the process was described as an aggression and rebellion against the inner voice, the practices themselves were pretty peaceful and I could arrange and sculpt them according to my life and morals. I quickly discovered, that it's much easier to achieve a great result, by reasoning with the inner voice, instead of suppressing and fighting it. For example, when I made the inner voice understand, that being organised and quiet is much more rewarding, than being all over the place and not getting to anything really.

As soon as the inner voice started to see, that being kind and understanding towards itself was much better in every way, then talking itself down. It quickly adopted a more positive tone. Even though it was still critical and sarcastic, it was no longer abusive and it started to adopt new perspectives quickly, as it understood, that doing so allows it to get to results much quicker and with much less energy waste than ever before.

Through some effort, that looked like this. I go through the day minding my business, but when I notice the inner voice starting to vent over something, I reminded it to be more understanding and to calm down. So instead of continuing to rage and waste energy on inner conflict, it remembered how good it was to let go and calm down, so it did exactly that. After some time, that way of thinking became a habit and no longer took effort to maintain. As that was done, life became much easier and clearer. First it started off by being able to remember things much better and focusing on something was no longer hard. I started to see things from new angles and it felt as if my brain was rewiring itself. It started to see things in a new, more organised and harmonious way, as I and the inner voice started to become friends again and that made going through the day pleasant and easy.

As I've already said, different sources refer to the inner voice differently. Some call it the Mind or the voice of Mind. Some choose to call it the Ego or the voice of Ego. I think that the difference comes mainly from what elements of the inner voice the sources take into consideration and what aspects of it are valued or talked about more and in what key. In my life I consider mind and ego to be essentially the same thing. At the same time I do see them as separate things as well. It really depends on the situation, context and to what result I'm trying to get, as in some cases, it's more practical or understandable if they're seen as separate and evaluated as two different things and in other cases, it's better to see them as one, to understand what is to be understood. I think, that it's more about how one chooses to see the world. If I was to look at the world as dual, and everything being separate. I'd call the mind and ego separate things and depending on situation, I'd look for which is the inner voice speaking. If I was to look at the world as a place where everything is connected on many different levels and in various different ways, I'd see all those things as one. My motive is to simply describe my experience and observations. Whatever I'm saying is not meant to be taken literally or for a fact, as the outcome of reading this depends completely on the intentions of a reader. To add another point of clarification of why my words shouldn't be taken for fact, is because each and every one of us understands the given text and all words in general in their own way. For example, for one God may be some figure who's looking over us in the sky and for somebody else, God may be the universal force that is all and everything.

Looking at the world without a negative lens felt great. Not aimlessly throwing around my energy and attention felt even better. With every morning that I woke up, I could feel more and more clearly, how my being was becoming whole again. I no longer talked myself down, I once again obtained my

positive outlook on life which I had once let go out of my reach. The energetic drive to do things, to experience and live life returned. It felt like all the holes that I had in my head and my heart started to heal. As they were in the process of healing and as some pulled themselves together, I started to crave more knowledge and experience that could improve my life as drastically as the journey that night.
Remembering all my goals, letting go of unnecessary ones and fixing some to be more true and in sync with my being. I felt the urge to learn and to apply the collected info on practice, to get to them and to do that as efficiently as possible.

I remember somebody said *"The road to wisdom, is the hardest and the most exciting journey one may undertake."* I cannot recall who said it. Matter of fact, I can't even remember if I worded it correctly. Doesn't really matter though.
To an extent, I agree with the quote. The road to wisdom is indeed hard, if you consider active learning, effort and working with steps and mistakes hard. Yet the understanding of possible rewards is already enough not to worry about the obstacles and energy it takes. On the other side, it takes some time to learn how to cope with so called failures and lessons. To be more correct, it takes some time to learn how to extract lessons from situations and not take them personally.
After managing my perspective for a while, to let go of the personal attachment to experiences and no longer take lessons for failures. I started to find a lot of joy in every experience, as I started to see how the same experiences are preparing me for whatever I want to do and are teaching me valuable skills and mental practices which in the future and in the very current moment as well, allow me to reach new heights and do things in a much productive way.

From that time on, I never felt as if something was a failure or a negative outcome. Everything was a valuable lesson and brought a lot of joy. Of course there were times and situations that really tested this new trait, but even the toughest moments were rewarded with great blessings, that taught the mind, that nothing was truly bad or negative. Along the escalation of this book, you will get to read my evaluations and deconstructions of those events, that in a way had put me through a lot of stress, while they taught me a lot and brought me many people and situations for which I am infinitely grateful to this day.

Along the lines you will get to see and maybe to an extent feel, why I've come to such conclusions and why I find them to be so grand, that I decided to dedicate a piece of my time and energy to write about them. As a considerably skeptical person, I think it's good, that you'll be able to read my deconstructions of those events as well as me describing how each step went down. You will be able to see, where I'm coming from. Plus because we all see things from different angles and no matter how elaborately I describe my experiences, you will receive them in your own way, based on your own experiences and understanding of life. From that, the conclusions I write are about are simply me describing my perspective, so if by the end of my entries or the book as whole, you'll find yourself having a set of conclusions and understandings, that are different from mine, it's also correct and good and should be neither dismissed or discredited.

URGING FOR NEW

My mental, emotional and physical states got better. I stopped drinking excessive amounts of alcohol from sadness and personal misunderstanding and started eating much better. Even though letting go of alcohol wasn't done at the right time. Ever since I quit drinking after I was hospitalised for 3 days. However, I don't consider that event negative, because it taught me a lot about my emotional problems, as well as how I should improve my diet. I stopped smoking cigarettes too. I obtained a clear understanding of why I was smoking and how badly it was affecting my health and performance. What really made me quit smoking on the spot was actually understanding how much it affected my performance in a way of not being able to run as long as I wanted to or not being able to sing my songs, because my lungs didn't have enough capacity. As I come from an athletic background, I could clearly feel how much damage was done in 5 years' time. Once upon that realisation, I threw away the cigarette which I was smoking in front of my parents' house and never smoked again.
I started to eat properly, more fresh vegetables, berries and fruits. I cut out processed foods like hamburgers and energy drinks. As I started to take better care of my physical and emotional bodies, my whole being boosted and with that boost, came a clearer desire to learn more as the things I've learned were the stepping stones that pushed me to undertaking those personal improvements. Therefore I and my mind understood that the more knowledge I obtain, the better results I can get and the easier I can get to them. It wasn't only about me though. As a caring person, I didn't care much about my own

wellbeing and grand results. But rather how the knowledge I was now able to obtain and use could benefit people around me and the whole world in general.

By now we can see, how that desire and drive is now manifesting in me writing this book, so even that is giving me a good feeling deep in my heart. Regardless of any accolades I may or may not receive.

Energy was flowing in and through me. I could feel the joy of being alive. Waking up in the morning was great and going on about my day was only making me happy. Not one thing could be bad, even if it was challenging. Every night I went to bed tired, but happy and eager to wake up to live another day. Literally every day turned into a possibly last day on earth scenario but not in the way it's often described. It wasn't scary or burdening, I didn't even think about it. It was simply that every moment of my day was filled with exciting activities, extraordinary people and interesting experiences. I started to look for authors and subjects, which felt interesting. I adopted a new way of finding things that fit me. Not saying that it always worked perfectly and that I never let ego or some emotion interfere, but the method felt the most natural. I trusted my heart. I walked around libraries and looked for articles, subjects and authors on the internet, hoping to find something that would resonate with me and offer me some material to digest and hopefully usefully apply in my life.
It happened so, that the books which I found interesting started to appear in book stores. Somehow the funds for those books found its way towards me as well, since at that the time I didn't have much. Matter of fact, I could barely pay for my food and rent and from that many funny situations arose.
Simultaneously, people started to come to my life. All sorts of people. Young and creative, new friends and conflicting people as lessons, spiritually gifted people and shamans. People started to enter my life in one way or another. Some came to me through friends and some came in the most unexpected

situations that made the meetings even more significant and magical so to say. All of a sudden I rediscovered spirituality in a whole new light.

Spirituality was no longer something outlandish and profound. It was no longer some weird thing my parents talked about, never really used and wasn't just monks meditating in mountains. I rediscovered spirituality in a way which was very present, real and physical. Spirituality became a way of life and a way of approaching things. It's not very different from what all of us do. It's just experiencing the same life we all experience, but in a slightly deeper and more understanding manner. It became my way of seeing and understanding things. The more I learned, the more I could do. The best part was that I could do things better. In every book I've read, I could find some information that shed more light on the questions that have been floating in my mind. More questions busted out of the answers that I found or understood along reading those books. The people that came into my life taught me abundantly as well. To be honest, experiences involving people have been the most outstanding. I got to learn about the great variety of people, who inhabit this earth and I got to learn a lot about myself. How I felt towards things and how I got irritated by my own issues, when I saw something in somebody else.

Something deep within was urging me to learn about spirituality and how it could be applied to life. The same something constantly reminded me, that the world I could see and feel was much bigger and much more mysterious, than I could ever imagine. I felt the desire to explore my inner world and all the selves that live and have lived inside of me. I wanted to learn about the great universe that was in and around me, that was me and that I was. I wanted to learn more about nature and how we coexisted with it. How we could coexist in a better and more harmonious way. As a result, this book and the upcoming books are my experiences with what that particular something told me to educate myself with. The results can be uncovered from between those lines and used for whatever purpose one may find fitting, if found fitting. Either way, I had great fun experiencing and writing.

The books started to stack on my shelves and the topics started to get more and more complex. From *"The 7 Spiritual Laws of Success"* it went to literature about metaphysics, psychology and biology. If I compared it to diving. With each meter of depth that I had adopted. My eyes had adjusted to the darkness and as I understood what was above me or on my level, I quickly noticed, that there was even more to explore below. The deeper I went, the deeper I could go. As if after entering a small hole in ice, I started to go down a tunnel that got wider and wider. More angles started to reveal themselves and the funnier it got. While thinking I knew more and more, I find out that relatively looking, I knew less and less. The craving for wisdom and experience started to play with my comfort zone. I could feel how my environment and my own skin started to feel too tight. It felt as if everything I've been doing was no longer productive. It no longer generated new results or experiences and turned into a pointless cycle of repeating patterns. Sitting at home no longer felt interesting. I wanted to do new things and go to new places. Most of all I wanted to meet new people and go through new and exciting

experiences. That tight feeling in my skin which I mentioned before, can be described as an itchy feeling within my skin.
As if I was not being able to sit in one place, because I've already had enough of repeating those activities. I needed something fresh and I needed something new, so I went for it.

I graduated gymnasium by passing the math exam with just 1 point. Lucky shot, because I solved one fraction of a problem, that was on the third page of an about 6-8 page long exam.
It's a funny memory to recall, but it doesn't hold much more value to it in my opinion. After graduation, I lost my job as a marketing manager in a restaurant. Besides that, it took me two months of continuous effort to receive my last check. While I was debating, reasoning and blackmailing (not in the literal way), I was living with Mick and his girlfriend. We lived in a luxurious apartment between downtown and airport. It was a historical building that also happened to have a restaurant, hair salon and a photo studio in it. We never went to any of those, because none of us had any free money. Everything we managed to make on our jobs was enough to pay the bills and buy some food. Not to mention that all of us had jobs, until I lost mine. We all contributed into paying bills and the apartments rent. In that apartment we recorded many songs, had many fun nights, long conversations about life and our dreams. The high ceilings and modern lights made the atmosphere very wide and open. No matter how many people were in there, it always felt spacious. Another beauty of the apartment was that there was barely any furniture and on top of that, we had two cats. In that apartment I had another spectacular experience which was also undertaken together with in the company of Mick.

THE SECOND JOURNEY

One day Mick offered me to go on another spiritual journey. I can't remember what was the reason, why Mick wanted to do it, so I'm not going to state anything. As much as I can remember, at the time, Mick liked to experiment with journeying to different states of consciousness and doing his daily activities or music. For the story, we can picture, that those could've been his reasons. Upon hearing his offer, I took some time to consider it. At the time I haven't had any scary or unpleasant experiences on my journeys, so I didn't think too much about negative scenarios, but as I've heard many warnings, I wanted to make sure that I was well prepared. The last time, I went on a journey in a very comfortable place where I was certain that everything was great. This time, I was in a fairly new place with a much wider spectre of possibilities, which could have gone down. I checked how much money I had to ensure that I had enough to get myself a ticket. Though I had enough for a ticket, what I forgot to consider in the rush of a moment was that at the time, my stomach wasn't in its best condition. I was fresh out of the hospital after my liver story. I forgot I didn't have enough funds to buy any proper food for the night.

Fast forward to the next day. We had our tickets and we were ready to move. We were home and as I said, the fridge was relatively empty. So was my stomach, even though I knew, that I had to eat properly and watch my diet, I didn't do that. Because I either didn't have the money or spent it on something more accessible. Mick's girlfriend was at work and she wasn't coming back any time before midnight or late night, so we had the whole apartment to ourselves.

We started our journey. We played some calm music and made our seats comfortable. We knew that the journey was going to take some time and that during the journey, the time would lose its value. We tried to prepare ourselves as good as possible with what we had in our surrounding.
It was a pleasant and calm evening. Nothing stressful had happened that day, so my mind was calm and I was ready for whatever, that was there to come. The first thing I noticed was how my vision became sharp again. The change in my visual perception was followed with an uncomfortable sensation in my skin. It felt as if my skin became super sensitive and all my clothes became uncomfortable, yet taking them off wasn't a good idea either, as I started to feel slightly cold. Though I noticed the uncomfortable sensation, I didn't make a big deal out of it. I just got myself a blanket and a pillow. On the way as I was bringing them, I grabbed a big glass of tap water. I got myself wrapped into a cocoon that I had made out of a blanket and laid down on the couch. It stood parallel to an identical couch, on which Mick was laying on.

I remember even after I laid down in a comfortable position, in a safe location, with a very close person, there was still something that didn't feel right. There was some sort of worry in me. It was deep and subtle. What made it uncomfortable, was that I couldn't understand it and I couldn't escape it. I remembered that it was important not to let negative thoughts get to me, as those had the power to change the whole journey to a very unpleasant one.
I tried thinking about positive things and bringing my mind to a better place. But it still understood, that the positive images, that I brought to my head were forced on and that there still was that subtle discomfort. As I laid there, my sense of time slowly drifted away. The uncomfortable feeling in my skin vanished, as though the uneasy being which was deep and

subtle was still there. I figured, that it was there, because I was holding on to something, but I couldn't figure what was the thing that I couldn't let go of. I was pretty successful at keeping my mind on a positive trail, even though from time to time it started to look at unnecessary negative scenarios.

One interesting experience that stuck with me, was that whenever I let my mind follow negative thoughts and started to feel worried or scared, Mick said, *"it's okay"* without even looking at me. I didn't say anything but I noticed, that he said that right when I was in the middle of a negative thought.

When I let another negative thought get to me, just as previously as I was in the middle of a thought, he had said peacefully: *"It's just a trip, let it go."* I didn't know how he knew, but I understood, that he could probably feel it. Or maybe he just knew. In a way, it felt as if we were connected in a much deeper way and could feel each other's thoughts and feelings. It felt as if that one thing, that brought everything to existence, was operating our bodies and awareness's as one. The negative thoughts didn't stay with me for long. After a while I got accustomed to the sensations in my body and the new width of my awareness which started to let go of whatever was holding me.

Next thing I knew, my body no longer mattered. It would no longer operate in the same way. My understanding of dimensions was crushed. The thing in my head, that understood where's up and down was, could no longer work. It felt like my body turned numb or as if it was extremely exhausted. It took infinite effort to operate it. The urges to go to the bathroom became more frequent, even though I didn't consume much water. I couldn't go against my body. I accepted what was there and started to stand up. Getting up turned out to be much harder than I had expected. Making my body sit up was a challenge on its own and as I got up on my feet, my whole world turned around. With every step that I made, the sensations in my body got weirder and weirder. I couldn't understand what I felt, as if one step I was drastically shorter and another I felt much taller. The corridor through which I had to go to get to the bathroom was narrow and tall. Two lamps were illuminating it softly and it felt as if I was passing through a futuristic cave, while being extremely drunk. The light in the bathroom was very bright, but my eyes didn't feel the burn. Everything was very sharp, yet slightly darker than it usually was. Taking a piss while not being able to stand firmly on my feet was challenging, but inevitable. On my way out I noticed a mirror. Seeing my reflection surprisingly reminded me that I had a body. I was too carried away by all the new sensations that I had completely forgotten about the existence of my body. Upon observing the reflection, especially the eyes. Something clicked in my head and an understanding got released into my consciousness. I was not the mind, nor was I the body. I was the awareness which possessed a mind and animated a body. I wasn't the one thinking or feeling. The true I was the one to be aware of the thoughts and emotions which emerged in its presence. I got almost childishly curious about that body and what it looked like. Especially the part that I couldn't see, which was my face. I looked into my own eyes, the pupils were big and black. Not demonically black like in the movies though. It's just that the pupils had covered most of my irises.

I didn't understand, why I had the body and why it was the way it was. The thought of it spawned even more questions. Why did I exist and what was the meaning of it? Why did the things appear differently in a different state of consciousness? Why did my ego disappear during the journey? I left the bathroom. I struggled my way back to the couch and wrapped myself into a blanket. Mick and I didn't talk much. There wasn't much to talk about, nor could we properly speak. We exchanged a couple looks and checked if both of us were experiencing a similar thing. Mostly, we just stared at objects and walls. I saw everything breathe. Something again reminded to me that everything was alive.

I looked at the walls and I could see them breathe. They reflected whatever I was putting out there. Then I noticed how other objects behaved in a similar way. I could see rainbows and bright colours dance on the walls and ceiling. Even though the lights in the living room were out, the bright colours illuminated the room in a seemingly impossible manner. Another thing I noticed about the lights and colours, was that bright *"happy"* colours made my body feel differently. It was as if the colours that were bright and pleasant— filled my body with happiness or energy and made me smile. Smiling itself also brought a similar pleasant and happy feeling. I figured, that in order to maintain a positive atmosphere, I simply had to carry on smiling. While I was looking at the ceiling, I saw many faces, patterns and picture. Some morphed and changed and some didn't. While I was watching, I noticed how my mind and the inner voice could no longer find their comfort. They were floating around my head and in my skull, trying to find their place. Something asked: *"Where does the mind start?"* They flew around, until I soon noticed how they started to wander off. Like a small boat, being pulled further away from the coast by a strong current. I was in that boat too. I got an uncomfortable feeling of uncertainty. Something wasn't sure, as if it wanted to let the mind wander away. Something told me, that at that very moment I could let go of my mind. Simply as that. I could let it float away and forget about it. For a fraction of a moment, the opportunity sounded interesting and I started to get curious, but then something told me, that I should not do it.

Before spawning an understanding of why I shouldn't let the mind go, something in me decided to reason. It told me that indeed I could let it go, but why would I want to do such a thing? Why in such a young age, while I had a whole social life in front of me? Another sensation came over me. It told me, that if I let go of my mind right now, I may not be able to retrieve it. I decided, that it wasn't a good idea. I had too many places where it could be utilised. I quickly pulled it back, secured it, and carried on observing whatever floated into my awareness. My first journey was pleasant. It opened my mind and told me that everything was going to be alright. Then the second one, was more challenging and was no longer luring me in. It was intense. It picked apart my old beliefs and showed me which ones were false or no longer useful. It opened my eyes, broke me down and brought me back up.

A challenge of maintaining my mind was passed and so it was time for the next one. Hunger started to poke at my stomach. As I hadn't eaten anything that day, the stings were rapid and sharp. The hunger was unbearable and caused even more emotional and physical discomfort. I decided not to be silent and shared my situation with Mick. We agreed on cooking something. As I said before, we didn't have much in our fridge and there was no money to go and buy something. It was too late to go to the store anyway, as the shops in our area closed at 22:00. Besides that, I wasn't in the right condition, to go out and seek food, even if I did have the money to do that.
We walked up to the fridge and started to look through its contents. I remember that we had four cucumbers, some eggs, a drawer full of spices and buckwheat. I put a pot of water on the stove and threw in the buckwheat, while Mick scrambled eggs on the pan next to it. It didn't take long for the eggs to be ready, so we threw them on the biggest plate we had. As soon as the buckwheat started to look slightly different from its first form. I took it out as I thought it was ready. Spoiler, it wasn't. The food was on the table and we were eager to eat. It smelled and looked nice and I was excited to dismiss the stabs which were attacking my stomach. I took a fork and shoved some eggs and half cooked buckwheat in my mouth and swallowed it. Instantly I felt bad. It felt like I went through the whole life of the chicken, that laid that egg and I could feel its pain. Still not feeling dimensions, I ran back to the bathroom, fell on my knees and let everything come up. As I was there, multiple sarcastic thoughts had crossed my mind so I laughed. When my stomach was empty and I no longer felt bad, I went

back to the living room. I knew that I couldn't go on like that for long, if I wanted to make it through the night without turning it into hell for myself.

I drank some water, to fill my stomach and got a cucumber for me and Mick. Laying on the couch in darkness, surrounded by ambient light and eating a fresh vegetable felt amazing. I remember thinking that a cucumber was vegetable water and I was so grateful for it being there, as it was the only thing I could eat. There were only two cucumbers that were available, so I stretched them out for as long as I could. I ate them slowly and drank a lot of water, to keep my stomach filled with something, so I wouldn't start to feel bad again.
It was dark and quiet outside. From behind the windows, we no longer heard the big stream of passing cars, that drove along the highway and the cats had turned up and were more active. The peak of my journey was over and we were quietly enjoying whatever we were experiencing. I remember how one cat laid on my stomach, as I was trying to calm it down after throwing up. As the cat laid down some warm loving sensation came over me. It felt as if the cat didn't talk to me, but communicated through some deeper understanding that arose from us simply being in the same room. The cat knew what was going on with me and it knew what was hurting me. It laid on that exact spot and in a split second, the pain was gone. For the whole time of the cat laying on me, I felt very happy and grateful for it being there, for sharing its warmth with me. After a while of us sharing the experience it stood up and left to mind its own business.

We laid there for some time. Mick and I started to have small conversations followed by prolonged pauses. The ability to compose sentences returned, so we began comparing our experiences. We quickly came to a conclusion that we were having a fairly similar or a common experience. We discussed what we saw and what it felt like. What understandings came to us and how we translated them. An interesting thing I noticed, was how different intonations and things we said generated different colours. Those colours then filled the atmosphere and crawled up the walls of the room.

Whenever we talked about love, happiness and positive things in general, while using an uplifted positive tone it generated bright yellow, red, orange and pink hues. The colours were easily separable and every different note and intonation changed the tones of the colours that connected some dots in my head. To test my theory, I chose to speak peacefully and only about positive things. The results proved what I had suspected. While I spoke peacefully, the atmosphere around me was bright and yellowish. I could feel, how my words vibrated within me, radiating into the tangible world of outside.

My attention was caught by the two cats which I had mentioned before. For the past couple of hours, they were fairly peaceful. Simply laying around on different surfaces while occasionally begging for food. All of a sudden, both of them ran to the exit.
A couple seconds later, I heard the door lock open and the knob go down with a fairly loud click. It was Mick's girlfriend.
The door opened quickly and just as quickly, followed by a bang it closed. The next moment, she quickly paced through the tunnel to the living room. The cats ran along, loudly letting her know that they wanted their food bowls refilled, even though they weren't empty. I don't remember what she said, but I can clearly remember, that she was very tired, irritated, annoyed and maybe to an extent angry. Neither me nor Mick understood what was the reason for such distressed? Whatever she said, brought deep blackness into the atmosphere. If earlier the room was lit without any lights, then now even with the lights on, it was completely pitch black. The other things she said, had flown from dark purple to black, then back to purple and deep dark red. We explained to her what was going on with us but that didn't change anything. That angered her even more. By that time, I started to feel tired and

wanted to leave the disrupted environment. I stood up, took my belongings and went to my bedroom.

Walking was no longer a challenge and my sense of dimensions was slowly returning. Though the outside world wasn't wild and weird like it was for several previous hours, the processes inside of me were still much in power. I opened the door and went into the dark bedroom. My room was in the back of our apartment, on the inner side and thus it didn't have any windows. The only source of light in that tall, yet small room was a lamp that gave barely any light and a candle by the side of my bed. I didn't light up the candle because going out of the room again, getting a lighter, returning to the room and lighting a fire was too much of an effort for me at that particular moment. I laid down and got myself comfortable. It didn't take long for me to notice the numbness, that was still present in my body, yet there was some different depth or level, that I could feel flow all around my arms, torso and legs. My mind was still wandering. I saw patterns in the darkness, as I couldn't make out any outlines of walls or furniture around me. Only a source of light was a small crack under my door. A very dim line of light was illuminating through the crack. That light told me that the sun was rising and the night was coming to an end. Simultaneously the same light reminded me that the journey was coming to an end. Besides that, the presence of that dim sunlight brought some sort of deep sensation of peace and relaxation. The patterns in my vision started to ease and the numbness that once took over my body was now fading away. At some point I had turned on my phones screen, to have another source of light shining in another corner of my room. The objects in the room that got some amount of light from the screen were no longer moving or breathing. From that, I concluded, that the journey was slowly coming to an end.

For the whole journey, I didn't smoke anything. From personal experience I got to learn, that I don't enjoy mixing. Along the trip, there were a couple moments when we rolled. Though the sharp smell alone made me feel uneasy, so I skipped smoking. I'd like to mention, that I'm not a person who journeys often or who does it for fun. By the time I started writing this book, I stopped journeying using external inducers at all. I discovered much more practical and less needy methods. The only outer force, that I keep as my close companion is trees. I don't mix them with anything else and when I do use them, I do it consciously. We'll get into that later. Even though I usually engage in daily interactions with trees, during those certain journeys I didn't. The different state of mind which is inflicted by the trees while already being on a journey, is unpleasant to me.

As the journey started to come to an end, I started to regain the awareness of my body, which was now enhanced. A wave of exhaustion washed over me and my eyes started to turn hazy, while all over my body I started to feel this subtle but pleasant heaviness. After being energised for a long time, the external boost started to wear off, while bringing the true tiredness. From behind the door I heard, that Mick was still awake. I heard some muffled sounds of activity coming from the living room. The evident sounds of crackling and plastic moving along wood, though I can't remember if I heard any music playing. A thought arose in my mind, it turned into a desire and next thing I knew, I was opening the door. I came out of my room. The space around me was no longer distorted. Rays of sunlight which came from the rising sun hurt my eyes a little, but the pleasant tones of it made the whole experience rather stunning. I felt grateful for being able to perceive dimensions properly again. It felt great to walk through the corridor. By the way, I can say that walking my way to the living room felt as if I was floating. I walked out from behind the corner, and in the left part of our living room, I saw Mick peacefully sitting behind his computer.

We looked at each other. A simple look into one another eyes, was enough to deliver an understanding of other ones wellbeing. Words were an unnecessary waste of energy. Walking barefoot on a slightly chill wooden floor felt amazing, I couldn't get enough of clarity and balance. I sat on a far right window. The windows in that apartment were about as tall as I was. Before them there was sofa sized windowpane made from stone and cement. The Cats and we loved to sit on those windows. Panes could easily fit several people, cups of tea and an ashtray. The view from them wasn't the most significant, as our apartment was on the backside of an industrial building. A cellulose factory to be exact. So the view that we got was an abandoned warehouse, a highway and a small fraction of a lake. Regardless, on that particular morning it didn't matter. Chill air, that came through the crack of the window was refreshing and reminded me of nature. The city was only waking up. The highway didn't have many cars on it, so even our surrounding was more or less quiet. I sat on the window, I brought out a small pouch and stuffed its contents into a grinder, mixing with some tobacco. To this day, I feel like the grinder that I got to use that period of my life was the best so far. The grinder did its job perfectly. All the contents were broken into small pieces and mixed together. A small piece of paper turned into a little tube which I carefully placed on the left side of a paper. After adjusting the tube, I poured the contents of the grinder into the paper. It took me about a minute to nudge the mix with my fingers into a small balanced tube and sealed the edge with my tongue. I no longer felt repulsed by smoking, but I didn't feel the desire either. I noticed it and analysed it for a bit, before lighting it up.

What I understood that moment, is still with me to this day. From time to time, I still go over the matter, in order to see if I've gained any new knowledge about it or if it has grown into something different. What I noticed was that smoking only relaxed my body a little bit, but didn't do anything to my mental state. I didn't feel the desire to smoke, nor did I feel any type of mental or emotional addiction. What I did notice though, was that it was more of a habitual thing. I wasn't smoking to get high or to get any answers. I was smoking because of a habit. Because between activities, I didn't have anything better to fill the small gaps with. As a result, I just went on with it. My mind told me, that it was less energy consuming, than stirring up the depths of my mind and starting to seek the deeper reasons for my *lack of personal love*.

As I lit the cone, the itchy sour taste touched the back of my throat and flew into my lungs, instantly filling my awareness with a slight haze. I held it for a second and naturally let it out with a small sigh. The journey was over. It was great and brought many experiences to me, that I now had to deconstruct and learn to apply. The journey gave me a new understanding of my body and how to communicate with it. That felt important and I made a mental note, to not forget about it. I shared a couple hits with Mick and we exchanged a couple words about our experiences. We were happy and tired. Agreeing that both of our experiences were stunning as separate, as well as one, and that there was a lot to learn about them. After a couple minutes, a burnt roach was all that was left of the cone. I put it out into a ceramic ashtray which I had placed next to me earlier and went back to my bedroom to get some rest.

LACK OF INNER LOVE

During my second journey, or the end of it to be more correct. I got to learn more about inner love and love for self. Many times in my life I had heard that happiness and love were found within. I heard that only inner happiness and love were true and that everything that brought us those emotions from the outside, was only there for a small amount of time. Attaching your association of love and happiness with those outer things is simply abusive towards those things and yourself.

For the whole extent of my depression, I didn't feel any love towards myself and my happiness was only there during certain acts or depended completely on things that were outside of me. Therefore I had no idea what was inner love and how it worked. Upon getting out of a pile of misunderstandings that was depression, I started to discover inner happiness and love through waking up and feeling eager to learn and do things. I started to feel it at all times, from simply being alive and witnessing whatever there was. Depression took a toll on me physically and emotionally. At first, it was hard to be able to see what in me wasn't as bad as the abusive mindset had taught me. I started to see that within me there was infinite love. I just had to notice it and let it come forth. In some areas of my life, I managed to bring it out, express and share it with people. On other levels not so much. For example why I'm still smoking herbs. It's because I have an inner idea of having so many things to do, that I don't have time to seek the reason of me choosing herbs as something to fill a gap in me. I do know, that eventually I will get to it and that if it becomes abusive, I will start handling it right away. But so far there hasn't been anything which would point me that way.

Back to the topic. Maybe somewhere along the book I will get deeper into the whole topic of Inner Love. The subject itself is pretty large and is good to know about however, in healthy balanced amounts. Right now I will say, that Inner Love is a very valuable resource of energy that every existing being in this world possesses. It's good to be aware of it and sometimes, to intentionally guide it. When we're not aware of our Inner Love, we tend to feel unhappy. We seek for love and happiness everywhere but within ourselves. This leads us to seek for security and love in money. To an unnecessary need for approval from others and many addictions. Addictions are usually the best and most visible example of lack of Inner Love. Any addiction starting from food addiction and ending up with fentanyl, all of them speak of the same thing on different scales. What they all have in common is that they all have a destructive nature and don't lead the person to any type of real wellbeing. Lack of Inner Love can come from various sources. Often it's an emotional trauma from childhood or teenage years, that wasn't understood or well received, so it left a mark. Not to get too deep into that, but it stays in the sub consciousness and brings us too many discomforts. Lack of Inner Love may also be programmed into ones consciousness and sub consciousness by social media or their community. When pressure is too strong, people often give in and let whatever there is to have the power over them.

The first step to recovery would be awareness, acceptance and understanding. Those three elements would allow a person to see the situation from different angles, shielding them from personal attachment. They will guide the person to deeper understanding of themselves and the source of their issues. Of course it all requires effort and mental energy. You still have to do the understanding and going back into those events yourself. To see them in a new more developed way.

Awareness allows us to notice, what's going on in and outside of us. It allows us to see, what things play a role in our lives and how they affect us. In a way, we can compare awareness to a very advanced device, that can tell how humidity and acidity (or whatever) within us affect our behaviour, productivity and wellbeing. Awareness allows us to become aware of our problems through a chain of processes. Firstly we want to notice what is going on in order to know where we're standing. Then we become aware of what we're looking for or where we're trying to get. Then it helps us to find the best way how to get to that result and what conditions inside of me need to be changed in order to get to the desired result.

Acceptance is another important step. We can't function properly when we're mentally beating ourselves up for every small mistake or misunderstanding. When we don't accept ourselves the way we are, regardless of being satisfied with where we stand or not. We are in a constant conflict with ourselves and therefore we lose a significant amount of energy on processes that we don't need and as a result, we lack energy that we could use for the actual work.
Of course in a way what I'm saying may sound radical, but I'm only bringing up radical examples to illustrate the matter with more contrast. Yes, we can get the physical and mental work done when we're in a conflict with ourselves. For example we can see many people who work in box offices or in customer service. Many of them are in a constant conflict with themselves and still, they get their job done. They get paid and they go home to do whatever they have energy left for. Now if we took somebody, who wasn't in a constant conflict with themselves and the person we previously talked about. If we make them both do the same or a similar task, regardless of their personal properties (as we can pick people as similar as possible. For example we can take twins) and the one who is

in balance with self, will perform much better and will be less tired in the end. To me it sounds like enough motivation to start accepting myself the way I am, in order to grow.

When we accept ourselves the way we are, regardless of us being or not being satisfied. We can clearly see where we stand and what's going on. That gives us the energy that we need to start inflicting the positive change within ourselves as we're no longer wasting huge amounts of energy on being in an unnecessary conflict. When we have accepted ourselves for the way we are we can start to appreciate the results we have achieved because they suddenly become good enough. Then, we can still acknowledge, that we are not satisfied with where we are, as wanting to grow and evolve is a natural and healthy desire. Growth is movement and movement is life. What is stagnant is dead or dying. So now we can start mapping out what do we want to change about ourselves or our surrounding, *(and by changing surroundings I don't mean cutting down trees and building roads, because walking through the woods is a hustle but instead, if desired one may find a better place for themselves by knowing, that they want to be in a place where they don't have to walk through the thick woods)*,

According to results we want to achieve.

Next important step that needs to be done before proper work can be started is understanding. I put it after acceptance, though those two can be the same or on the same step, as one comes from the other and vice versa.

Understanding allows us to truly feel and deeply know, why something had happened and what is there to do with the results or opportunities at hand. Understanding helps us to notice the balance and reason behind chaotic events and processes that to a casual mind seem incoherent. Let's not forget the saying *"As above, so below"*, from which we can conclude, that if the mind sees things as incoherent and chaotic, that means the mind is incoherent and chaotic. Thus projects these properties on what it sees. Understanding allows us to see and feel with certainty. If something is right for us or not. It helps us to uncover the deeper truth behind things and if we really need, then to change things drastically. Or if we just need to let go of a certain viewpoint or an attachment. With understanding often comes compassion and feeling of love. Those *"side effects"* so to say, are already a mark of improvement and progress towards the result we're trying to achieve, which is abundance of Inner Love.

When we're not aware of our lack of Inner Love, we are vulnerable to many dangers and abuses from the outside and inside worlds. When we become aware of it through desire or just circumstances pushing us to that understanding. We regain the ability to influence our inner world and thus influence our outer world. In a way it allows us to liberate our lives from traumas, stresses and programmed thoughts, that we were given by many sources, consciously or by accident. By consciously I mean people being programmed by media and by accident, I mean parents projecting their fears and problems onto their children. As a result, corrupting their kids without meaning them any harm.

THE MORNING AFTER

When I woke up, somewhere around noon or maybe a little past it. I felt rested, but very hungry. I leaped out of my room in a rush of morning energy and went straight to the fridge. I was hoping to see some food magically appear and satisfy my ill stomach. Now to be honest, I don't remember if I found any food that was truly good and refreshing or I ate some leftovers just to fill my stomach. Though there was one, thing stuck with me to this day. All of a sudden I was very aware of all the processes that we're going on in my body. I knew exactly how foods affected my being. Which foods energised and filled me with nutrients. How the living energy of a home grown vegetable filled me with wellbeing. With that, I could also feel how white bread was nothing more than stuffed matter and how sugary were other store-bought foods. I'm a person who likes sweets. In the past I used to put a lot of sugar into my teas and coffees. Then that started to change.
When I ate something which was not fresh or was processed a lot, for example deep fried. My whole being shifted into something I could describe as short term sickness. I felt sick in my stomach and in some way that is hard to explain, my awareness felt and understood deeply. How bad are processed and modified foods for my physical body. The experience prompted me to change my diet drastically. After being hospitalised for half a year I couldn't eat properly. I had episodes of vomiting that could last from three to five hours, right after waking up. It was unpleasant yet turned out to be a very valuable lesson. The new awareness in me made me understand how unhealthy my diet was. The process began

immediately. I started to choose my foods and ingredients more carefully checking their sources and contents. Started drinking more water and consciously treating my body with natural foods that could improve its being.

These new discoveries were interesting. I was grateful for feeling them and was eager to use the new sensations to their full extent. I wasn't sure if the feeling was going to wear off with some time or not, as it could have been a come down side-effect. A memory rang in my head, reminding me that whatever was experiences through external help, wasn't going to last. The possibility that the improved sensations I had, could disappear any time made me hungry for a way to induce the same feeling or state of being from within.

Another thing I got to learn from my dad and some other spiritual people whose opinions I value and consider is that journeys and plant teachers may bring us to higher understanding and show us many things we've never thought of before, but they can only show us. During the journeys, our access to those things is very limited, as many are not trained to use them. What they all had said though, was that all of the things, that can be seen during journeys and learning sessions, can be achieved through various meditations and practices and when they were achieved naturally, the people who achieved them could access them at all times simply by desiring that.

WHY DOES ONE JOURNEY?

So far I've filled some pages with my recollections and deconstructions of my experiences that I had undergone while journeying in different states of consciousness. As my own parents are quite radical towards any plant teachers and any consciousness altering substances, I couldn't help it, but take it into consideration while writing this piece.

As the book started with a journey and some elements of journeying will have a couple appearances in the upcoming chapters. I would like to clarify something. So far in my life, there have been a couple of experiences with journeying. They were a part of my path and I appreciate their help. At the time when I undertook those journeys. I wasn't in the best place emotionally, mentally and physically and that could have been my souls cry out for help. To break down the ignorance in me.
Indeed the journeys were of help and gave me the enlightenment I needed to start developing and balancing myself properly. Now that I'm writing this it's been a long time since I undertook a journey with any help from the outside. Nowadays I feel completely fine going into my journeys through pure desire or meditation. I chose my first journey to be the introduction to this book, because it seemed engaging and entertaining enough to keep you reading until I got to say something valuable without dismissing it by sounding boring or delusional.

I don't promote the use of plant teachers or other substances. I'm not claiming that they are the ultimate solution to any sickness or disorder and most definitely I'm not saying that they're good for recreational entertaining use. If one desires to go on a journey. I highly recommend doing a lot of research on the subject and every element which will be with you on your journey. It's very important to be clear and honest with yourself about the reason, why you want to go on the journey and what are you trying to see or experience there?
Based on personal experience, I would also recommend doing it when you're in a good place with your consciousness and have some people around who are close to you or at least are experienced in guiding you through the journey.

Disclaimers and warnings aside. I simply want to say, that if you got an impression, that this book is about tripping and nothing more, then it's not quite accurate. Those experiences from which I started the book were simply that push that made me move towards numerous experiences, realisations and enlightenments. Those experiences and my descriptions of them are simply an entertaining element which hopefully makes the book more interesting and maybe much more relatable. Plus it gives an insight into my world and where I come from with the material that I bring to you through this work.
If it happens that you really don't enjoy reading about such experiences, then much as I remember, there's only one more to come and its story is rather brief. So hold on and take it simply as a small illustrative element in the book. You don't have to attach yourself to it. If you feel like it, you may skip it. The choice lies within yourself.

WATCHING THE TIME

Time went on but it moved differently. According to my memories, the last time it moved that way was when I was a small child. Before I had any responsibilities, programs or unnecessary worries in my head. My mind was free and it felt light, like a small cloud of fog moving along a field. It came and it went but at the same time it was always and never there. I couldn't touch it, I couldn't feel it. I couldn't even know if it really was there, but then again I could. How else would I know that I exist right?

I could see the dates change on my phone, but essentially nothing and yet everything changed. I could still recall the social elements of that time I picked up and adopted along my path of life and education. My mind was still making attachments to times and dates. Somewhere deep within, something started to tell me that it was not that important.
How could time not be important you may ask? Or maybe not. Maybe I'm just eager to talk more about time. Time is important to an extent. It's limited. Someday we will die and that is inevitable. Time is important when you arrange a meeting with someone in your social circle. Time is important when you have to make it on a certain plane, to get to a certain location on time. But time is not important when you're asleep. Time is not important when you're taking a walk in the forest or when you're swimming in the sea. Yes the mind may have attachments to it and it may make it seem like it's so very important.

Deep inside though upon deconstruction, we could all see the so called *"time"* as we know it, is only a tool used in society. Birds don't care if it's 09:00 or 16:52."

The new understanding of the concept of time started to sink in my being. I didn't force it down, nor did my being push it away. Naturally, it started to become a conscious part of me. Maybe my lack of a job was what helped me to adopt it quickly and without any stress. In this case, as I didn't have to wake up early in the morning or stress about being fired for one reason or the other. I could wake up whenever I wanted *(which was usually at 07:00 - 09:00)* and started doing what I wanted straight away. I didn't need anybody besides myself, to experience or write. Nor did I need anybody, to meditate or go out and influence the world. Time slowly ceased to exist, until a need for its utilisation arose. I needed to know what was the time or a date, only when I was trying to work with somebody or wanted to go out with some of my close friends. When I started waking up early and living my life partially without time. I started to notice, how late many people woke up and how I myself used to wake up in the late afternoon. I saw how much potential energy and time to be active, was wasted by me going to sleep late and waking up even later. In a couple weeks, time was no longer an anchor to me. I was free of time and could utilise its aspects whenever I wanted to. I woke when I wanted to. I enjoyed waking up early. I had the whole day and night, to do what I desired. My biggest desire, was to develop and create.

The desire to create has been in me since early childhood. As a kid, I had a wild imagination and was passionate about drawing. Later the imagination faded and I adopted graphic design. Later I picked up songwriting and music, with which came along my current form of writing. I was creating as much as I could and as well as I could. I created by myself and with other people. I found new ways to connect and to have fun with it, but still there was a small inconvenience. I didn't have any money. My roommate didn't have it either, even though he still had a job. At that time, the only actual money provider was his girlfriend. She worked in a house that was a restaurant at daytime and a bar at night, so her shifts were long and well paid. Now that I'm looking back at it, I don't think it was embarrassing in any way. If anything, it was just funny. From her side, it was very sweet and kind.

As my skills and potential grew, so did my cravings for new experiences and achievements. I wanted to do more, to see more, to give and to get more. But, I was broke. The things that I wanted seemed expensive and my outlook on life was still too narrow to look for actual solutions. Instead I felt sorry for myself and constantly ranted about it

When I set aside complaining and understood that it was not going to help me in any way, I sat down to meditate. I tried to find answers or clues for how I could start making more money. How could I make money, with what I already do?
After about an hour of sitting up with my legs crossed, slowly breathing and not talking in my head. No answers came to me. All I can recall happening, was me simply sending out a desire.

Before we go on, I would like to talk about being sorry for ourselves. Even though I talk in a form of "we" or "us", what I'm saying is based only on my experience and my observations, so I can't claim anything to be a fact. About being sorry for ourselves. When we're being sorry for ourselves, it means that our ego thinks that it's important and that what it wants must be given. Thus it can't accept the reality as it is and therefore chooses to conflict, complain and throw childish tantrums instead of accepting the reality as it is and starting to look for a way how to solve whatever it is that doesn't make you happy.

NATURAL TIME, THAT IS AND ISN'T

Natural time is the nonsocial element of *"time"*, which exist and doesn't exist freely from us. Natural time doesn't depend on our existence. If we ceased to exist right now, the sun would still rise and rivers would still flow. We just wouldn't be there to witness it with our physical eyes. We ignorantly think that everything requires us to function. When in the current reality, we're the ones that require everything to function ourselves.

Natural time is and isn't, as to us it exists only because we are able to notice it. We happen to be the animals that are able to notice how things flow. With our narrow yet productive minds we decided that time is linear. Then we made some use out of it. Animals don't think about time. They go on doing their things, trying to survive and carry on reproducing. Birds don't care about the time, they don't attach themselves to it. They just know when to fly to the next location. In a similar way, plants don't care about what time it is. They grow regardless and have their own practical methods to sense and know when to act for the best results. In some ways we humans have managed to adopt this primitive practice but not without abusing it. As much as I observe the escalation of time. All that matters is what processes are going on and where they're moving. The rest is just details and gibberish.

SOCIAL TIME THAT WE MEASURED

Saying that we created time wouldn't be correct. Saying that we gave it value and started forming our lives around it might be a bit more acceptable. As previously mentioned, time is and it isn't. We just chose to see it as something which is important and started using it in different ways. We use time to schedule meetings. To let others know when we're active and when we're asleep. We use time as a measurement and we use it as an excuse or an argument.
We often don't have time for this and that is because all of our time is occupied by the importance of this or that.

When I got unemployed, the social understanding of time lost a major amount of its power over my life. I no longer had a place where I forced myself to be. I didn't have to run around, trying to get tasks done on time. I didn't have to worry if my pay-check was coming on time. The checks were not coming because I was unemployed and in its own way, it felt nice. I'm not saying that not having money felt good. No. Money is a part of our social world and it brings comfort. It's just that I no longer felt the burden of an unpleasant job, that didn't provide enough anyway. I no longer had an attachment that would bind me to the consuming concept of time. I didn't have any more obligations. Now I could see, what it felt like to be empty. To be clear. That gave me the opportunity to choose, what things I wanted to attach myself to. I remembered my childhood. The only attachment I had, was that I had to be home by sundown. Then I got followed up by episodes where somebody had pushed the attachment to time into my head, either in school or in some other situation. At that time, I didn't know any better so I let it get to me. Nothing is permanent. One of a few valuable things which can be extracted from our understanding of time. So with that, I looked at those episodes in a new light and learnt. Those attachments that I once let people shackle me to be, were no longer suitable for my life and it was time for me to let go of them.

To bring more examples. I'm going to describe some of the attachments, which we bond ourselves with. The type of attachments that are connected to our concept of time and abuse our mental and physical health in a very subtle, yet evident way. Again to be clearer, I would also like to mention, that the concept and understanding of time itself is not abusive or unhealthy. It just is. Not being aware of it and still attaching ourselves to it on the other hand might turn out to be abusive.

For example: You wake up and look at the time. You instantly remember todays date what happened yesterday and what you have to do today. You don't get to wake up properly and be in peace for a moment. Soon as you wake up, you drag yourself into this social life where time is of utmost importance. And then you wonder how can you always be tired?

Another example: Imagine yourself waking up on your birthday. You just turned sixty. There are more summers behind your back, than there are yet to come. Some happen to get anxious and start to regret that they did or didn't do something. Then they marinate in their own negative thoughts and emotions instead of looking at where they've gotten. If desired they could even changing something in order to make some steps towards improvement, that is still within their reach.

Personally, I feel like time doesn't matter. It doesn't matter what time it is, what day of the week or what year it is. What truly matters is what you do with the time at hand. How aware you are of it and how you let it affect you. The rest is just minor details which hold any importance only in certain circumstances or under certain angles.

ADOPTING THE FLEXIBLE TIME

Time goes by, flowing like a river. Always the same, yet in depth always different. Every morning I woke up with joy and a feeling of bliss. Of course there were stressful days when morning peace was disrupted quickly by the urgency of social responsibilities that I had taken. Every morning was different from the previous one. I looked slightly different, felt slightly different and my position on my path was different. In a way, every day felt like a cycle and yet there was always something odd and mysterious.

I broke down my previous understanding of time and learnt it in a new universal way. By that I mean the understanding of time turned from linear to flexible. Where point A and B are the same but from different angles and there are many variables.
I started to see clearly what my balance of time was or better to say energy that I had for the day. Depending on my physical and emotional states, I knew where the energy could be directed. Adopting that was an experience which changed me for the better. I can't describe the relation between the things I'm going to describe next and yet I can feel them being connected in some way. If it won't make sense naturally, hopefully somewhere along the book I will be able to break it down better.

When I adopted the new flexible understanding of time and started to pay attention to my inner voice and physical body. Many aspects of my mental and emotional state started to improve. For instance, I've never had good memory. Even being a musician was difficult in a way as it was hard for me to memorise my own lyrics. In the past, I wasn't good at focusing on a task and getting it properly done. Plus I was messy overall. What happened next baffled me. I tried to understand the relation between things that had happened, at the time I didn't come to a certain answer. Later I made peace with it and just took it for something which simply happened. So far I haven't thought about it much, because there hasn't been a need for it. So what happened, after I applied the changes to myself? Well first of all, my overall emotional state changed. As I became aware of my stressful attachments and false beliefs, I became able to let go of them. As I let go of them, a lot of headspace and energy freed up which probably led to the next improvements. I started to focus better. As I had more headspace and awareness, I could see what things were worth focusing on and what weren't. With that understanding of what was truly important to me came the ability and energy to focus on those things. The most significant improvement I would recall, would be memory. With a lot of freshly freed headspace, I could remember everything that held any value to it. I could remember all the phone numbers that I needed for as long as I needed. The door codes, passwords and directions, all easily stood in the back of my head and popped back up as soon as they were needed. As much as I've deconstructed the improvement in my memory. I've come to a partial conclusion, that it happened because I could differ important things from unimportant ones and unimportant ones simply faded away.

NEW FISH IN THE POND

A few weeks before we had to move out of the beautiful apartment which I still get nostalgic about to this day, I started to notice myself around new people. I've never been the type of a person to change my circle often. Matter of fact, to this day I stick to the same people with who I started the conscious journey of life. So to me, a change in my surrounding and an income of new people is very notable. It felt as if a bunch of people were sent towards me to teach me lessons and offer new opportunities. What is interesting is that the people that were sent the closest to me, didn't stay for long and taught me only a few minor lessons. The people that are now closely related to me and will have many appearances in this book, were always on the side away from the spotlight but always had some very nice energy to them.

As the new people came into my life some offered great opportunities musically, which taught me a lot about the craft and the industry which had impressed me as a teenager. Though they gave a lot to my creative side. They weren't meant to teach me about getting what I truly needed, as they didn't have it themselves. While with them without even noticing it I started to interact more with the guys that didn't like the spotlight. Our meetings became more frequent and the tones in our voices became friendlier.

Even though I was very outgoing and social, they were always very content and quiet. At the time, I didn't understand it and took it for awkwardness, but soon I learnt, that it was simply them being careful. They were living a lifestyle, to which I was soon to be introduced.

The energetic exchange between us became stronger and more consistent. All of us, as well as the universe saw, how the new alliance had a great potential and was in the right place at the right time. Funnily enough, aside of the time and place being right, we had a lot to learn and experience. The new lifestyle was about to test me, to see if I fit in or not. On many occasions I had caught myself thinking that my life was very much like a movie. There have been certain events which could easily be turned into bestselling movie scripts. Gladly I started to notice how every day that had passed reminded me of another action movie. If all my previous years were rather basic and overused introduction to a cheap drama. Soon it turned into a full blown plot twist filled with philosophy thriller.
I had restored my hunger for life. I was eager to jump into the unknown and find what I was looking for. I had the energy and dedication. I knew that I had to learn and experience a lot, as my goals required many skills, connections and most importantly, applicable wisdom. The universe as I like to call it, felt it. Things I had no knowledge of shifted and all of a sudden, all my interactions with the people made sense. All of those moments were a steps of introduction. Though at the time, I didn't pay attention to those steps. In the end of that chapter of my life all the dots had connected and became a clear picture. The universe shifted its elements and I had met with the guys again, but this time under new circumstances.

CHAPTER II:
INTO THE UNKNOWN

One nice and warm evening in August I was casually spending time down town. The sky was turning yellowish as the sunset was approaching. That evening I didn't have any plans so I decided to meet with the guys before I went home. I didn't have much money and I was looking for ways to make something, to pay my bills and afford good food. I've always known that Ian and David didn't work regular jobs and that they had a very interesting way of making money of which I didn't knew before. Previously our relationship wasn't close enough for me to ask, how they made their money. Our relations surrounded music production and were mostly work related.

I met up with Ian. That day, our meeting wasn't the same as the other ones. It felt like he knew or somebody had told him about my need to make money. As soon as we met the tone in his voice was more excited than usually. He told me that he has noticed how frequent our meetings had become and that our paths are becoming paralleled. He smoothly implied that as I have a lot of free time and don't have a steady job maybe I would be interested in joining them. That would give me the opportunity to make some money and get it more frequently than once a month. I've been introduced to different preliminary *"opportunities"* before in my life. When he mentioned quick income, I started to pay attention more carefully. I was aware of the abundance of free time and the fact that I needed money but I wasn't willing to waste my

valuable time on running around bringing money to some enterprise that promises me a manner. Though only if I reach some certain heights, nothing of that type was interesting to me and I was more willing to keep looking for other ways. He noticed the change in my being and asked if I had any questions or if I needed any clarification?
I asked my questions and he explained to me that the business was fair and I was interested because I was already doing something similar. Joining forces would make us all more productive and valuable. He explained to me that as I was already in graphic design and knew many interesting people around town, I could help them promote their imported coffee beans. As they were young entrepreneurs just like many of people I knew, I had some feeling that it had a chance. Plus it also happened that I knew people who owned or were related to cafes so I could make my profit even quicker than expected.

On that note, I told him in a more positive tone that I also had some experience in marketing since I've worked for a restaurant as a marketing manager in the past. He figured that I was interested and then proceeded to explain to me what I had to know to be able to make my efforts more effective. I went home with a good feeling but there was also a slight nervousness present. It felt like a small weight on my heart which was coming from fear. It knew I was going into the unknown and far out of my comfort zone. I brushed off the nervousness and decided that I could overcome it by simply planning out my moves and reading articles on the internet which could educate more. It was exactly what I did upon arriving back home, I rolled a slim tube and opened my laptop. Found about twenty tabs of content and started scanning for valuable info. All the different strains of coffee and how they could be roasted. How the smell changes depending on conditions and how different grinds affected the flavour of the coffee. Since I loved coffee anyway and used to drink a lot of it on daily basis, I thought I might as well educate myself on the subject and start drinking good coffee.

And so I did my research and collected the contacts of people I was going to meet the next day. I was introduced to the business just one day before the next order was made. I didn't have much time to do any preparations. I went to sleep late that night as I wanted to be as prepared as possible. I was focused on obtaining new knowledge about coffee, as well as some tips on psychology and communication, hoping it would improve my sales.

Here I would like to mention since my second journey which I undertook in the apartment, in which I was doing the given research on coffee beans, that it was the first major instance where I was introduced into the importance of the lesson I experienced during my second journey. The one where I saw lights and colors shift during conversations. In a way it was always in the back of my head and I was actively but lightly trying to apply it more in my life. Then I saw, how it could affect the efficiency of my work and how much I could make.

ENERGY IN THE VOICE

When I was talking about my second journey in an altered state of consciousness. I talked about the change of colours and atmosphere as similar to when Mick's girlfriend entered and started talking in a negative tone. When it was happening it left a big impression on me. It made me feel so uncomfortable that I understood that I never wanted to make anyone feel the same way. No matter how subtly the effect manifested outside of the altered state of consciousness I knew that during the journey, the whole experience was very visual and affected many of my other senses. Awareness of those effects stayed with me. Long after the journey had ended and I had returned into my casual state of mind. In the so to say *"normal"* state of awareness. The effects are still there, but very subtle. They still affect us emotionally and therefore physically, we simply don't see it visually.

From the end of that journey, up to that very moment. I was aware of the energy in my voice but the knowing was very subtle and it was stored in the back of my head. I was able to access it and I was actively trying to apply it in my life but as the need wasn't that evident. The efforts and results weren't as visible either. I tried to pay attention to the way I spoke and how my voice vibrated. I tried to look as deep as possible, into what words I used and what intentions they carried. I wanted to know thoroughly. How I could use my voice and vocabulary like a tuned instrument rather than a broken radio? It was an interesting thing I noticed about my life. Whenever I joke about life being easy or something having no use, if not instantly then quickly enough the Universe finds a way to turn that joke into a lesson. If previously I had mentioned, that there was no evident need for application of that knowledge then through playful gestures of the Universe. It swiftly became my primary tool for making that bread. It was no longer a fun thing to watch and just try to apply for slightly better outcomes. It was now something which played an important role in my daily life and had a straight impact on the results. The results in that case were important, as they were able to give me what I needed for growth. It was now something I had to actively utilise in my communication with people. I had to use it wisely to make it as efficient and honest as possible. As a somewhat spiritual person *(at least I consider myself to be)* and also a person who has worked a lot in making promotional campaigns and commercials. The idea of planting a desire into someone and selling it to them conflicted with some of my beliefs. I wanted to approach the matter carefully, so I wouldn't abuse it or inflict any bad karma. I wanted to be effective and honest and do the promotion work towards the right people. The ones that needed the beans could get them and the ones that didn't wouldn't get them force-fed.

The experiences had taught me, that my voice was a very powerful tool. Most of us have it and the ones that do, are actively using it. Some of us know about its power and are using it with awareness. Others are simply using it to the extent that they're aware of. As a result, the ones who know about it and use it get to their desired results. The ones who don't know are being actively used and milked by the ones that do.

In a way, it may sound unfair but the world is the way it is. If that causes you to be unhappy then the only working way I've seen would be next. You can become aware of things that affect you in an unpleasant way and change yourself into what you believe to be more fitting. If used properly it can bring great and lovely results.

If used out of corrupt intentions, it can bring distress and self-harm. It was now time for me to start actively using described knowledge. I didn't know how ready I was but I couldn't stay in a state of preparation   forever. After all, it was going to show me whether I was taking a step in the right direction or another stumble into nothingness.

CAREFULLY SCAMMED

I woke up early. My head was clear and I knew exactly what I had to do. It was the 18th of August. A date that will stay in my memory for a long time. That date changed my life quickly and drastically. The change was unexpected and thrilling.
I could never label it bad or negative as it brought me the most valuable lessons and experiences to my life. It introduced me to some of the most amazing people and put me on the right track on my recovery and growth. Matter of fact, that path became so exciting that it provided me a lot of material for this book. Also many valuable life lessons that I now use daily and will most definitely teach to my children.

As I was eating my breakfast on one of the couches, mentally I went through the whole day. Through every conversation, I thought about the words, I was going to use. Even put in the extra effort, to think what would be the most optimal way to get to the locations I was about to visit. After finishing my breakfast, I sat back on the window. The warm rays of sun playfully heated up my body as I threw another pinch of herbs into the grinder and rolled the wheel. After three hard spins, the wheel moved smoothly. It was time to move on to the next step. The act happened every morning, slowly turning into a small ritual. Every move and act was precise, focused and rehearsed so many times it required no mental energy to complete it. Still every step was done with understanding and a clear intention. Just like cleaning up the surrounding can aid clearing out one's head. The ritual was something which aided me in my preparation for the day. I inhaled deeply for the last time, a slight burning sensation hit my lips indicating that there was nothing left to smoke while keeping my lungs shut. I put out what was left of the stick.

I picked up my bag, once again reassuring myself that I was ready. I started walking towards the wardrobe, everyone else was still asleep, so I kept my steps quiet and tried to make no noise at all since I got used to waking up early I was the first one to get up. I quickly learnt how not to annoy others while I mind my business.

There was always something special about being quiet and subtle. Since I was a child, I preferred to walk quietly. My parent's house had three sets of wooden stairs that made a cracking noise whenever pressure was applied to certain spots. Whenever somebody was going up or down it was clearly heard and felt vibrating throughout the whole house. For some reason, I always wanted to avoid that while at the same time I still wanted to get around fast. A little attention and childish curiosity helped me understand what spots created noise and which ones didn't. After a while, I learnt to get around without making any noise. When I was walking around the woods or gravel roads I noticed how certain types of shoes interacted with the surface and how much noise they generated. Feeling that I adopted my steps to the surface. It didn't have a real purpose at the time. It was just something fun. Later on, when I started to move around more often and got to live in different places, especially the time when I had roommates with drastically different personalities, I started to notice how making noise, leaving things around and simply doing too much created a lot of unnecessary noise and hustle.
For example: leaving things around made the place messy. Not taking care of dishes right away created grease and dirt. Using your roommate's items without putting them back created misunderstandings and sometimes conflicts. People also happen to be very different. I wake up early and I'm instantly in a good mood and ready to do things. Many people wake up late or are not very social during their first hours of being awake which made me learn

I softly closed the door behind my back and set my steps
towards the stairs. I jogged down the stairs and proceeded to
walk through a red industrial corridor that had some modern
art placed on the walls. It reminded me of a transition between
levels in a game. From a cozy and peaceful place that I could
call my home I was making my way into a huge social world of
interactions, business, relationships and more. I smiled at a
possible neighbour who was entering the building and as we
were passing greeted each other.

*I always try to be social with my neighbours and people who work in
the area. On one side it's because it's pleasant to know what nice
people reside around you or what stories are going on around you.
On the other side, it's also practical, as maintaining a healthy
relationship with the people around you may bring out many
opportunities and benefits like discounts and being able to pay later
on as a sign of people's trust in you.*

Pushing open the heavy glass door was like the small effort I
had to do in order to go out into the bigger world. The first
fourth of the push was hard as my body wasn't yet used to
work and I didn't put enough effort into the push in the first
place. The rest of it was easy though. The magnet was no
longer holding the door, so it went smoothly. The first thing I
could feel was a wave of hot air that hit my face, and sunlight
that hurt my eyes for a brief moment. The heat was quite
pleasant and rare in our area. My eyes adapted to it quickly so
I didn't make a big deal out of a seemingly drastic transition.
My wrist slid in my pocket, grabbing the phone and a set of
headphones. I plugged the cord into the phone and after the
headphones in my ears. A hip-hop playlist seemed to be fitting,
as the quick drum patterns were energising and lyrics ignorant
enough to put me into a more motivated mood.

Before attending all the meetings I wanted to have a cup of coffee, so I went to a local coffee shop and ordered a cup of Latte. While waiting for my beverage I browsed through my phone. It didn't take long for the beverage to arrive. I took a couple of small sips and started messaging the people who I was about to meet. Some people were quick to respond and some took time. The scheduling was done and I set my feet towards the direction of the meeting locations leaving the half empty cup on the table.

Many people I met that day were excited about my offer, yet slightly suspicious of me having such a good and quick opportunity at hand. It was not something casual in those parts for people to have good offers and be willing to hand them out. Of course some saw it as a possible scam and refused quickly which back then slightly got to me. I brushed them off and continued with people who were engaged enough. I explained to them how the offer worked and why it was good. The explanation was simple and honest enough to make them trust me even more. I collected the money for the order from people who were on board and carried on to the next procedure. I collected a good amount. The guys were surprised by what I had brought. I counted the money and put my profits into my pocket. I took a picture of it as a memory of my first good income. At the time I thought it was a good thing to do. The rest of the money that was meant to pay for the order was put on the table. I listened carefully how the rest of the night was going to pass. We sat down and placed the order. Some time had passed and something started to feel off. I didn't use any of the profit money as doing anything with it felt incorrect until the people who gave it to me were satisfied. The guys started to get worried too. The opportunistic investors so to say started to question the honesty of my words. They messaged and called me trying to figure out what was going on. I've always tried to maintain a good name, plus the business I was trying to get into required me to be honest, clear and correct. So far I was known as a nice hard working person who was creative and willing to help many.

I started to notice the signs of doubt in the eyes of the ones who trusted me, and in some cases I started to hear tones of aggression in the voice of others. Some even got to the point where they threatened me. When about seventy percent of the people got worried, I felt that it was time to act. I met up with the guys and asked them about what was going on. Ian, the one who I've labelled as the put together, business-minded one, looked at me with a slight smirk. In a very calm and friendly tone told me that it was an *interesting situation.*

My heart sank. A hundred bad scenarios flashed in front of my eyes. In the middle of my head I could almost feel the escalation of every possible outcome that could be spawned by the words Ian was about to say. It wasn't too long after I had eaten, but any sensation of satisfaction had disappeared in an instant and a hollowing feeling of deep emptiness had entered my guts. Turning it into a bottomless hole. The pause lasted only enough for him to take a breath and look into my eyes. In my perspective the moment had stretched to an enormous length. It seemed like another journey but with a very unpleasant twist. Where it wasn't just emotional and physical discomfort anymore but there was also danger. We were standing in a small parking lot next to a mall. The air was cold and small bursts of wind blew chills across my body. With the corners of my eyes I could notice groups of people passing by, cheerfully chattering about the upcoming night. Summertime Fridays are loved in this area, it's the time when locals can drink and party without any worries. More and more people came out of public transportation making the town more and more crowded. The amount of vehicles decreased leaving mostly cabs and government cars on the streets. It seemed like the whole city was getting ready to go out, leaving all their workday life behind. The time had stopped at the parking lot where we stood. I was told, that we got screwed over, there were no beans! The backstory didn't matter anymore. Nor did the reason.

The validity of that story had no value to it anymore, as it being true or false didn't change the fact, that we did not have what we promised to provide. During the speech that Ian delivered a couple more young entrepreneurs joined the circle of our audience. I heard the story over and over and with each time, it got clearer to me that the words I heard carried no meaning whatsoever. Like Monopoly money the words were thrown around. Just sounds which had no practical application to them.

The whole incident turned even more cinematic when a folded piece of paper was pulled out. It was a standard piece of A4 which had a message in black ink written on it. The first thing I noticed was that the handwriting was clean and lines of text were very straight. The handwriting was rehearsed, the sentences thought through and letters were written with precision in a peaceful atmosphere with plenty of time. I read the letter. It was a stale apology. It was written as if it was supposed to be presented by an actor in some mediocre Hollywood thriller as an explanation to why the character did what he did. The letter didn't create any emotions in me. It was just text on a paper. Nothing more than an excuse or an attempt to make the person feel better.

I asked Ian why he let this happen. As I had understood, he had experience in this business. How could he let this happen? The explanation was fair and as I've been treated in a similar way before, I could relate to it and no longer hold anger for Ian. He told me that the person who had bamboozled him was his old friend. He had trusted him for a long time he added, as if he had worked with that person closely in the past, he had no reason for doubt and so everything evolved into the situation we were in. The past no longer mattered. While I listened to him explain what had happened, in my head I had already gone through every moment, that led me to that exact moment. Now I had to accept it, I had to admit that out of a desire to get out of debts and a poor financial situation I had acquired an even bigger debt, which could potentially get me severely injured or even killed.

I felt a bit of fear, but mostly I felt sorry for myself. Every second of excitement I felt returned to me and laughed. Every last bit of expectation had crumbled. What I had wanted the reason why I got into the business, it was now times further away than it was before. I thought to myself that if I continued the way I was going, I would have gotten to the result eventually. Maybe with a bit more effort, but nevertheless I would have gotten there. Now I was in an even bigger mess. I was now in a debt of six thousand euros and potentially getting killed. I've heard many stories about how in these streets, the worth of a life varied from fifty to two hundred euros. My situation was times bigger than that. Business here is also heavily observed and taxed.   We hadn't registered our business yet, so the police wouldn't help us either. They would have probably screwed us even more for being active without a registration. Now standing in the grey area, between completely clear legal business and fairly criminal activity with no protection or a way out. I understood that it was now time for me to take full responsibility for my actions and become a bigger man than I had ever been before. The whole meeting took us about thirty minutes. We didn't have any more time to waste. The customers were ready to meet us and were expecting to get their product.

We shook hands and I left. I went to the heart of the old town, I sat in a corner of a dark alley which the only visible light in my surrounding was a window. I could see an elderly man sit behind a sewing table. He was working on a piece of clothing. His face was calm and focused. I could see in his eyes that he was passionate about what he was doing, and all the years that he had invested into his beloved craft had turned him into a happy elderly man with no worry or fear in his energy.

For him it was probably just another night, no different from any other one which he had experienced during his previous decades.

Yet the most valuable thing I could see in his eyes, was the loving knowing of peace and safety. As soon as he finished his work he would probably go to his warm home, to his wife and children and their grandchildren. He would eat something his home had prepared for him with love and would fall into peaceful abyss of sleep later. For a moment, I came out of my reality and entered his. I could feel his being, I could be him in that very moment. It felt calm. The split second of peace reminded me of the contrast of my situation and snapped me back into my body. The emptiness in my stomach was present again. Once again I felt sorry for myself. I didn't know what to do and I wanted to cry. I tried to push tears out of my eyes. I thought that pushing out everything that I had in me would empty me out and help me in some way, but tears didn't come and feeling sorry for myself only pulled time, like gravity pulls the grains in a sand clock.

In my heart, I felt that the situation wasn't right. There was a knowing that I had to fix the imbalance which I had created with my desire for money. Giving up or running away weren't options that I was even considering. Those things were always against my morals. Of course I could always cancel something or no longer pursue a certain path if I could feel, that there was something deeply bothering me or being in a dissonance with my heart. But in no way I could sleep peacefully with a knowing that I had caused distress and not put in the effort to resolve it. I wasn't raised that way. I accepted the situation the way it was and let go of being sorry for myself. It didn't work. There was no practical value in continuing to waste my energy on nothing, when the situation was this serious. It was time for me to start thinking in a new way and there was no better time for it than that very moment. I brushed off all the negative scenarios. I started to think how I could ease the tension between me and the people who had trusted me? It was not only about the money but by the way I present myself as a human being. I decided to call every person one by one.

The ones that were close I arranged a meeting with, and ones that were further away, got to feel frustrated over the phone.

I still had the profit money that I had not spent. I pulled it out of my wallet and recounted a couple times. I had spent a small amount of money on some tools. That made the tension in me grow a little more as I had gone against my morals hours earlier and now I was seeing and feeling the unpleasant aftermath. As I was meeting those same people in a now very unclear and intense situation.

In the middle of the night on a day, when everybody was expecting me to provide I applied every particle of my attention and every piece of experience I had acquired in the past to resolve the conflict as peacefully as possible. In that case some of my past actions had plaid along. When I was thinking, and who I was going to approach personally. Most of the people were my close friends or people I've known for a time. The people I've surrounded myself with were not violent, slightly impulsive at most. I being an overall polite person who's always been up to help provided some sort of comfort to people with whom I was conversing. It resulted in no violence and people relaxed a little. It took me a good three hours to meet every person and explain to them, how I had messed up and how I was determined to restore every lost cent. Though I promised everyone that I was going to make it all back for them, deep inside I knew that I wanted to give them more as to better the stress I had caused. It was something I thought about but didn't speak of. I no longer spoke of things that weren't present or confirmed. I could no longer waste words. I could no longer afford it. By the end of the night I had no money left. I had given away everything I had and my virtual balance was now negative six thousand euros. I walked through the whole city that night, which upon recalling looked like a scene from a movie.

Three am on a Friday night in our city is the time when everybody is wasted. Groups of drunk people swarmed around twenty-four hour kiosks and fast food restaurants which happen to be open until four am on weekends. Some drunk loners stumbling around the streets trying to find something to strive for which is usually a nice looking lady, their friends, the next bar or a way back to their place. At those hours, the shouts in the city center are more incoherent and sirens go off more frequently, than on other days. Our locals love to yell and get into unnecessary conflicts. They're drunk and need an outlet for their energy. Tourists get too drunk and scream for their companions. The night city is beautiful, except the slightly saddening sight of too many drunk people and not enough activity for those people to replace getting drunk. My hometown is small. Throughout the years it has grown and improved, while maintaining its medieval look that made it so special and outstanding in the first place. It takes about twenty to thirty minutes, to get from one end of the city to another and it takes about two hours to cross the whole country by car. The busses don't go around the city after midnight, nor does any other public transportation. Probably the lack of people and nightlife makes it more reasonable, to not have the busses go around at night. Maybe it's the greed of our politics, but that's none of my business. Cabs are relatively cheap here, though not having any money was still a pretty heavy factor. I thought to myself, that it usually takes about fifteen to twenty minutes by bus to get where I was headed. On foot it shouldn't be much longer. The only comforting thoughts were that I have walked longer distances in worse conditions in the past. At least that night my sleep was somewhat secured. The steps were heavy and my being uneasy. Accepting the situation was only a fraction of the whole situation, as I had to provide results and ensure the people that I haven't disappeared.

It was my first time being bamboozled in a relatively big way and I was taking it to sleep with me. Moving further from the city center was like leaving a slightly crowded bar street. Music faded and so did the voices. Only a few cars passed me by, with the majority of them being occupied cabs.

To be honest it didn't even matter if there was any noise or not, as the outside world was muted during that walk. Everything that I looked at reminded me of the situation, ringing and hitting the back of my head. Most of the houses were dark with only a few windows being lit. When I looked at them I couldn't help it but think how people slept in peace. How nothing in the universe mattered to them as long as they were deep in the abyss seeing dreams or floating around the endless spaces. Recharging their mental energy and resting their body. The overall seriousness of the story, that I got myself into at the time made me say goodbye to sleep. I could feel how countless restless nights full of moving and risking were in front of me as I had to fix which I had caused. When I looked at the taxis that passed me every now and then, I thought about all the drunks and workers, who were heading to their nests. Some of them satisfied with what they had done, some of them less happy. Though I didn't think that many of them could be going through what I was going through. My situation seemed so specific and different that I couldn't imagine anybody else going through it. Back then it seemed to me, like that was the moment I had seriously fucked up. I remembered my parents and how they had told me about similar situations. It was funny and sad at the same time. It humoured me because I was in that situation. The slightly sad part was that I didn't want my dear parents to worry. They are great people and I have infinite love for them. They have worried for me enough in my teenage years. I wanted to spare their nerves and hearts from such stress. It took me about forty-five minutes to get to my destination. I got back to my resting place and I looked through the fridge and eat whatever I could find. After stuffing my mouth with food I brushed my teeth and laid down. It took me a while to fall asleep. The time that it took to get there wasn't the most pleasant transition from awakened state to sleep.

Before passing I made an agreement with myself. I wasn't going to spend any money on my minds desires until I paid everything.

The sleep that I got wasn't the best. I didn't feel too rested upon waking up and the exhausting thought hovering over me, reminding me about the heavy lesson I learned yesterday.
I allowed myself to take my time with breakfast and getting ready. If I was going to spend most of my time out there trying to make money, I might as well go prepared. I finished my breakfast slightly slower than usually and then opened the messenger and the first message, that reached my inbox before dawn was from Ian.

He offered to host a big meeting with all the people involved, so we could figure out how we can resolve the case. The message said, that I should notify him as soon as I was awake and come to the location he was going to announce upon replying.
About half past noon, I arrived to the city center. No money in my pockets. I stood around the same area where the news got broken down to me. The meeting location happened to be in the park right next to where I was. I was one of the first people to arrive. The park wasn't the best place for a meeting like that so I offered Ian to pay a visit to my Turkish friends.
I gave them a call and asked if it was cool for me to come over with a couple of acquaintances. To drink some tea and have a quick chat. The reply was positive. We arrived onto a nice cozy apartment with a park view. It was small, but large enough to fit in all of the thirteen people who were affected by the inconvenience in one room. I made tea for the people who wanted it and we started discussing our options. Firstly I was surprised to see so many young people being honest and responsible. Everybody paid attention, spoke honestly of their situation and was willing to help each other. Nobody ran away, as soon as the problems came up as I somewhat expected. Instead everybody decided to get it resolved. When everybody

finished talking about their losses we started a new discussion about how we could get it resolved the quickest. I won't get into the details of that conversation as they don't hold anything that could make the story more interesting or valuable.

What I will add though is that during the whole time we were talking.

I could feel peace sink in me. I could feel how I was surrounded by responsible people and that it wasn't even important if they helped me. I could observe and learn what to do myself. After finishing the informative brainstorming we decided to get to know each other a little better. We knew that we were going to spend a lot of time together and being able to communicate well between each other was a crucial part of our work. When we chatted up some individuals. I once again learnt that those people were much like me but so very different at the same time. The whole negative aspect of the situation was slowly fading away from my mind. An idea of that situation being an introduction to a completely new lifestyle arose. For a moment it felt like the whole occurrence was hosted by the Universe to test me and see if I was willing to think in a new way, in order to get what I wanted.

The previous day was no longer a stressful nightmare. I was grateful for it. Accepting it and letting it go of my attachments to negative aspects of it made me realise what a big opportunity and a pool of lessons it was. The Universe had answered my desires in a very unusual and straight forward way. That day I learned that there are no bad or negative situations. Situations simply are the way they are. It's my perspective and inner world that put labels on situations. Becoming aware of that was another realisation which changed my inner and outer worlds for the better.

NO GOOD & NO BAD

Everything that has or has not manifested in the physical reality simply is or is not. Sounds like a weird metaphor from some novel or movie and yet if understood and perceived to depth It can reveal some great lessons about life. To be honest even the lessons that the understanding may provide just are and aren't. They are there if you notice them and not if you don't. The understanding has power and can bring results if used practically in one or another situation. Therefore has no power to it at all if just kept on the shelf.
"As above, so below", has no use unless understood. I've heard it for years but it's been only months since I understood it to some extent and learnt to use it for my benefit.
To illustrate the significance and simplicity of the subject. I'd added an example. What's the difference between life and death if there's no one who would experience it? Or what's the point of life if you don't do anything with it? Something doesn't matter unless there's something that could experience it. Light is just a word different from dark when there's nobody whom could experience either one of them or put them into perspective.

In those two days, I had my first lessons on the subject of how my perspective affected my world. What happened had taught me that every situation regardless of how social programs label it has potential in it. The potential can be noticed and realise by me depending on my perspective and what is my desired result.

For example: For many and at some point for myself as well, the situation that I had described earlier would be very embarrassing, scary and stressful and in general negative for them. Indeed I felt all those emotions in the beginning as I didn't experience such things before. The situation taught me to learn quickly.

After feeling the negativity fill my body and stress me out without bringing any results I understood that it wasn't something worth of my energy. I also noticed, how in the past throughout my whole life. I've gone through many stressful situations that worried me a lot at the time of their presence. Then when they were resolved or time had just passed the same stressful things were gone from my heart and my memory like a short summer rain leaving barely any trace of it. But why would I feel stressed out and waste my energy in the moment, if I know that in the end, I will be feeling good and will once again see that whatever bothered me wasn't that bad. Why can't I just feel good right away and pursue changing or working with the situation in a better way?
I thought about it for a while and it made sense. Not wasting my energy and utilising it properly and looking at everything with a positive outlook sounded in a way better. At that point I had nothing left to lose, so I decided to try it. The results turned out to be stunning. It was my first major situation from many where I had tested and applied this type of understanding.

I thought about the results I was striving for and how I could pursue them in a positive way. Quickly I started to notice how many different visions started to pop up in my head. Clues on what acts would bring the nicest escalation of events and results. Then I started to notice how opportunities started to come out. Soon as I understood what way I should go it felt like the opportunities that had spawned out of nowhere went right through me. Completing themselves simply through my intention. The situation was no longer a problem. It was simply there. It was more of a challenge or a game. As soon as the stress fell off the shoulders of others. I started to see, why they really did what they did. I started to see the beauty of the business. It was nothing like the stories that I had heard about. It was a completely different romantic and thrilling experience.

Yes, it had its own grains of salt but so did everything else. I was surprised by the contrast of my new lifestyle. It was quick and silent, fun and risky but at the same time very positive because somehow the kindest people happened to be around me.
It was great to feel that no situation had the same amount of power over me like before. Any negative situation could be turned into a positive one. Every small thing can be grown into something bigger. As if dimensions of everything had expanded.

Now let's put the story aside and look at the chapter in a way we could extract something practical out of it. The title says *"No Good & No Bad"* and it can be understood in a variety of ways. Simply speaking nothing is really good or bad. Situations just happen and things simply are the way they are. The mind is the one that chooses to label everything. Besides putting misleading labels on things one sees it also attaches itself to whatever it reaches and makes the person feel many abusive emotions. Right now let us discuss and deconstruct the subject as simply as possible. In the upcoming chapters, we will look at it in depth. For now, let us save ourselves from the possible confusion and an overload of information.
So let me explain how I find this information practical in my day to day life. Judging and labelling things, attaching myself to expectations and allowing emotions to take control over me never brought me significant results. Of course, when things went the way I expected them to, it felt good whenever I got to the results that I was striving for. The rewarding sensation felt great. Coming from that I was living in a world of duality. Being

drugged by emotions of joy brought suffering with it. I felt sad when things didn't go my way and I felt hurt when something didn't play along to my desires. Soon the negative emotions started to overpower the positive ones and I started to feel out of balance.

After reading few books and doing some research and meditation. I figured out that as long as emotions had control over me, I couldn't function properly or utilise my full potential. Evaluations brought me to an understanding, that if I distanced myself from emotions and observed their origins. I could free myself from their shackles. It took some time to learn how to apply the new theory, but after a while it became natural.

If you look at situations, people, objects, subjects, emotions and anything really in third person. You'll be able to see all those things from many new angles and without being attached to emotions. Essentially what that does is, that it allows you to experience whatever you're experiencing much more clearly and makes it possible for you to operate with a much bigger variety of choices. To simplify even more, not being attached to emotions and distancing yourself from your mind saves you a lot of energy and headspace. Allowing you to function better and become more practical.

A Simple Practice:

1. Take a thought or a memory that creates unpleasant emotions.
2. Become aware of the emotions that are created by the given subject.
3. Become aware of the place from where the emotions are coming from.
4. Without fighting the emotions without blaming yourself or others, accept and feel the emotions that are there.
5. Now try distancing yourself from the subject and your emotions. Try seeing yourself and the situation from a third person point of view.
6. Now look at yourself, the subject and the emotions that are created. Are they worth it? Is the matter serious enough for you to be so caught up in those emotions?

The whole ordeal with being bamboozled was resolved pretty quickly. It took us from two to three weeks to return everything we had lost. I grew accustomed to the new lifestyle and my marketing skills and new understanding of perspective allowed me to start making profits quickly. Now I had money and people I could make money off of. Surprisingly I ended up with more contacts because of getting everything back in place, instead of losing the ones who I had seemingly failed. Apart from that I had gained something I've never had before. A team of loyal people with an outstanding outlook on life. What made me appreciate the whole experience even more while it was showing me how being responsible for my actions in any situation made people trust and respect me more. Even if I had messed up the fact that I was responsible for it and got it fixed. People noticed it and it installed some sort of deeper trust in them. Not backing away not only saved my life but improved it in many ways and taught me a bunch of valuable lessons. I was now ready for a totally new chapter of my life and one of the most exciting ones so far.

The night had rewired my mind into thinking in a new pragmatic way which then had benefited me greatly. Being sorry for myself became somewhat a side effect that was easily manageable and no longer the main reaction to things. I was no longer doubtful or uncertain in my capabilities since I witness it with my own eyes on how I can handle situations when I'm really motivated to do so. The motivating sensation which I started to call *"the impulse"* became something that I could evoke in myself and utilise whenever in need. The impulse became more visible and tangible when I understood that in order to go into action and solve things, the mind and body needed to use a lot of energy. It never wanted to do that though, because the mind is in some ways lazy.

The night taught me how to get around that laziness of the mind and how to call for the impulse whenever the heart or soul felt it to be necessary.

THE IMPULSE

When I first started to feel *the impulse* in the center of my chest it felt like a small spark or a pleasant outburst of adrenaline. I'm not saying that it was an outburst of adrenaline but it's the closest thing I can compare to the sensation in order to illustrate it. I didn't know what it was right away or what effects it had on my body and surrounding. I had barely any idea, that it was strongly connected to my thoughts and that whenever I used it without the proper state of mind or preparation it exhausted my body like excessive amounts of coffee. Then I didn't feel the big difference as I was only getting into it.

What I found out was, that the impulse was somewhat of an additional property of my heart. It could be evoked in need through concentration. It was like a push which led me to action and simultaneously did the same by pushing the desired reality towards me. What it also did which I did not notice in the rush of joy and overwhelming amounts of opportunities was that the impulse pushed everything into stronger and more harmonious motion. The backside of it was that I was utilising a lot of my own energy without being aware of it. Putting away sleep in order to be active longer and accomplish more tasks. I had brought my physical and mental states to the point where everything seemed incoherent and chaotic. I was nervous and tired. I no longer could clearly see my goals or the purpose, of why I was doing the things I was doing. To be clear I could remember my purpose was and why I was doing the major things in my life. But the small things became hazy and unclear. I understood that the impulse shouldn't be abused. I should use it only in need or when necessary and even after using it I should rest properly and feed my body well. Using the impulse loosely took a toll on my health. When the damage was done I could only see how I shouldn't have acted and abused the new knowledge.

With time my body healed and my mind became clear again. I learnt that whenever my mind becomes incoherent and body starts to feel tired. It's time to stop working. Especially when the mind goes chaotic. When it is in that state it can't function properly and the results aren't as practical. Now I'm using the impulse only when it's needed or when I need to boost something in my life. Most of the time I don't use it or remember about it. The memory of it comes to the surface only in need.

A RANGE OF OPPORTUNITIES

The new circle of people that was surrounding me was exciting and full of life. It felt natural to be in there, though being out of my comfort zone conflicted with that natural feeling for a while. The new environment was so interesting and vast, that the first weeks of being in the new business. All I did was research marketing and psychology in order to be better at it. The memory of being scammed became our inside joke that to this day makes us laugh. I was grateful for what had happened and for what it had brought me. Those were the exact things I've been wishing for right prior to the events. It was a sign, that I was on the right path and that great things were waiting for me.

It took me about two weeks of continuous research, study and socialising with people in that field to learn the basics and some insights about the business. I felt confident enough to start doing it full time. Attaining the knowledge and doing research was a very basic thing to do. Being in a somewhat serious business even though with not that serious people I wanted to sound as believable and certain as I possibly could.
The whole business was very appealing to me. I had all the control over my time and efforts, which is what I wanted to have. As an early bird it fit so perfect that I could start working as soon as I woke up and finish whenever I wanted to. Additionally to that, I could learn a lot more while making good money than ever before. I quickly found people whose products and services I could market. Automatically I found

some more individuals and businesses to whom I could provide the given goods and services. It didn't take much time to see how my dedication started to pay off. People were coming to me from both sides, asking me for help. I could ask for whatever payments I wanted and could ensure people that results were on their way. And they did.

Besides just marketing, my social skills and the people I had found had given me the ability to be a middleman in many different businesses, simply because I was moving around a lot and interacted with many people. I knew who was into what business and what sources were available to them. Having that knowledge I could make profit off of connecting people. A door that had opened in front of me kept on giving and improving its opportunities and I was there to reach out to every one of them.

I had never seen that much money move around me before. Maybe I had mentioned that before getting into the business I didn't even have a wallet. Well as I got into it I felt like a wallet was a necessity in order to respect money and keep it nicely folded. I was quick to notice that when you have money, a wallet is pretty much unnecessary. The money doesn't fit into it. On a daily basis, hundreds to thousands of euros moved through my hands leaving some paper in my personal pocket. My wallet became a bulky leather bag of pocket money. The real money that I was working with needed something more simple yet effective to hold it together. Later I started buying rubber bands.
I once watched a documentary about Pablo Escobar. It was said, that he had spent a large amount of money on rubber bands just to hold his money in place.
Handing those amounts of money taught me a lot about responsibility. It was mental responsibility and a physical one as well. Many different people of all ages trusted me with their money. For some it was their free investment money, for some it was more of a personal risk they took in order to break out of

poverty. Some gave me their savings and some took out loans in hopes that I would help them. At first, it was compassion and understanding of the struggle that made me responsible, as I didn't want to cause anyone any problems and wanted everyone who worked with me to be happy. I couldn't let myself be at peace knowing that if I didn't do everything correctly somebody wouldn't be able to pay for their apartment or food.

Another thing that stimulated the growth of responsibility in me was the point that it was always relatively big money. At least on our local scale where there are places here where life is worth about a two hundred euro bill, I didn't want to owe anybody anything. Subconsciously I've always wanted to be appreciated, respected and to be seen in a good light. At first it was the ego, then it became more of a convenience that allowed me to do my things more fluently. The last important bit that shaped my responsibility was that I wanted to be the person who always got everything done well.

I handled things as professionally as I could. Usually I made sure everything went as smoothly as possible and if there were any complications I made sure they got resolved. In so to say, *extreme cases,* where things went missing or something happened to somebody. I put in the extra effort to resolve the difficulties as quickly as possible. My morals didn't allow me to let people suffer because of me. That had created trust between me and my customers. Extreme cases that happened from time to time also contributed in enforcing our relations. Of course some couldn't bare it and left or fell off, but that didn't matter. I was now a young man, who was relatively known and most importantly trusted by influential people.

For some time everything ran smoothly, with only a couple of minor obstacles or inconveniences that we came across. There were no problems, no conflicts and not a single bad emotion between us. My personal funds started to grow rapidly. I was actively progressing with my life and seemingly there was no stopping. As my pockets started to fill with money, I stopped worrying about things which used to eat at me. At first, the feeling off the fear of not being able to feed myself properly and then the fear of not being able to pay my rent. I knew that I could now always make enough to feed myself well and make enough to cover all the bills and utilities with ease. Eventually, I stopped looking at the price tags in shops and grocery stores.

Not because I had so much that I could buy anything with my eyes closed but because I knew that I had enough to buy everything I really needed. Knowing myself to some extent I knew that I didn't need too much. I didn't need fancy accessories or expensive clothes. I didn't have a driver's license nor did I cared for cars in general. Hence there was no need to spend money on a car or gas. In our area, cabs are relatively cheap, especially when you take into consideration the fact that the city is small and getting around doesn't take much. To waste a couple lines, I can get into a little more detail and add that as our city is small and central area is busy and filled with various colourful places. The parking here is expensive and hardly available at all. Therefore having a car would be much more expensive than taking a cab anywhere at any time.

Having money was like looking at both sides of the coin at the same time. It solved many problems and took away many worries. It opened many doors and simplified countless daily routines and more irregular situations. Having money made life easier. To an extent it made it more pleasant too since many things that used to weigh over me were no longer there to haunt me. I could say, that they were muted by money. Then again, money didn't make me happy. It doesn't take a genius to figure that out and yet many of us are blinded by having it or even by just following its trail aimlessly. It took me about two thousand euros to get that certain deep understanding that money was a mere tool for creating comfort and not a substitute for happiness. Happiness is something much more casual yet we often mistake it for being distant and out of reach. Happiness for me, is something I feel whenever I wake up, because I'm alive and I get to experience many exciting things I've brought upon myself. Happiness is learning, doing, and in general simply being.

DOING TOO MUCH

While I was meeting many people who I could label as my customers I rarely met other people with similar services to mine. I'm not saying that there weren't any around. Most definitely there were many other young businessmen and older wolves around. I just didn't encounter many for some time, because I guess there was no need. The team that I was a part of, was sophisticated and all around well built. Everything was thought through and there weren't many situations, when I would need to ask somebody for anything. I was comfortable.

What happened once in the past came back around again.
First it started by dislocating me from my comfort zone. The people who were responsible for some of the steps, were either busy or unavailable. I wanted to do more. Even though I had everything I could possibly need and relaxing for a moment, would have been the go to solution, I ignored it.
I started looking for ways I could go. Sliding my finger across the screen, I accessed my contacts and started scouting for people, who could be helpful or have any info about anybody, who could provide me the services I was searching for.
It didn't take long to find some people I could message. I opened the chats and started copy pasting them the same message, asking if they could assist me or if they knew anybody who could. Most said *"no"* but one young man said that he had somebody who was trustworthy and could find me the things that I needed. The young man told me, that he has been working with that person for a while now and that the

81

person to who I was being directed would not do anything out of the ordinary. I believed him, I had no reason not to trust him and the atmosphere that was surrounding the young businessman was relaxed and pleasant. I decided that I wanted to meet that person. I was eager to work more and be more versatile with my options rather than stick to the ones that were truly trustworthy and tested.

The next day came along, I did my routines, had breakfast and as I was preparing to light up the first doink I unlocked my phone. There was one orange notification bubble and it was right next to the young man's username. I pressed my finger on his name and the next window opened. The messages said that as soon as I had the money he was ready to arrange us a meeting. It was still pretty early so I had a whole lot of time to prepare the funds.

Excitement was slowly circulating through my body, rising to my head, though I was trying to keep my mind still, excluding any thoughts. The ambient sound of a working engine, accompanied by a subtle vibration which usually stayed in the background were more present that moment. The sky was painted into a soft orange, peach-like colour. The sun was setting again. My eyes were following the clouds. I was observing them, trying to see something hidden. Maybe a message from my sub consciousness or perhaps a sign from the sky.
I was looking for something. Most of my work happened during sunsets and still, each and every one had impressed me in a new way. It was something that made a grim looking suburbs more colourful and special. Grey and orange block houses and towers were mellow yellowish, mixed with orange and occasional rays of sunlight. It made me feel peaceful and brought joy to my heart. We passed a couple bridges, drove through narrow streets, surrounded by Soviet era houses until a highway led us to a gas station. My friend stopped his car a couple meters away from the station. Shutting down the

engine stopped the monotone vibration and everything went still. We sat quietly for a couple minutes while some old rock band was playing in the background. The quiet ambience was interrupted when my friend asked me if it was going to take us a long time. I looked to my left and asked the young businessman who came along with us and repeat the question in Russian. He said, that the person was a couple minutes away and that it was going to take an hour maximum. I translated what I heard to my friend and the silence continued. After a couple minutes passed a black BMW drove into the parking lot and stopped a few meters away from us. A bald man came out of the navigator's seat and started approaching us. The young man who was closer to him approached first. They shook hands as I was walking out from behind the car and shook hands as well. He introduced himself and so did I. I asked him a couple of questions that now seem completely meaningless. His replies didn't ring any bells in my head. I asked him too if he knew how much time it was going to take. He said that it could take up to two hours. For a moment I thought to myself if I was willing to trust somebody completely new with the money I didn't own. Something inside of me told me that I shouldn't: It was possibly greed that made me stretch out my hand to the person as I saw him take out a stack of money out of his pocket. Even my friend had said that he didn't have that much time to wait, I should have taken it for a sign that I consciously ignored. I gave the money to the person and went back into the car. I told my friend about what happened. I could see it on his face how his mood slightly changed as I told him that it was going to take more time. He agreed to wait with me.

An hour passed, so did the second and the third. My friend told me he was no longer able to wait and that he had some things to take care of. I got my bag and signalled to the young man who was waiting with me that it was time for us to exit. We sat at the gas station for another hour waiting for news. The sun was now down and it was dark outside. I was slowly growing impatient and the messages on my phone blowing up. Muting my phone didn't mute my thoughts. Neither did it shut down the worry which was slowly boiling in my heart. The small cafe that was built into the gas station started to shut down and we were asked to leave. It was cold outside and the nearest gas station that was open for another two hours was a kilometre away.

The mood wasn't the best and something was now telling me that I shouldn't spend any money on transportation. We agreed to walk to the next station, waited there for some time and then see what we shall do. I was trying to be as optimistic as possible. Excluding any negative thoughts and trying not to manifest anything bad and yet something in my heart was telling me that things were off. I smoked my last doink in the back of the station. For some reason, whenever something of that kind happens to me the circumstances around and prior are always very trashy and ratchet. I went back inside and sat in front of the young man. Asked him to message the person with whom he had made me meet and ask him what was going on. After waiting we were told, that there were some minor complications that were about to be resolved. They ensured us that nothing was off and that we should continue waiting.

Another hour had passed and we started to call the person more frequently. We spammed him with messages until his phone went offline. At that point I no longer had the same optimism. I was now expecting to be ignored, until a bitter realisation of being bamboozled was going to sink in. It was a bit over midnight when we decided to split our paths. Agreeing on contacting each other in the morning as we went home. I wasn't in the mood to catch the last public transportation and I didn't want to spend any of my money on a taxi when I had messed up. I set my feet towards down town while a bitter process of deconstructing and analysing was going on in my head.

After a bit of walking, the rain broke loose. The air turned colder, as the night was progressing and the rain turned to sleet. Bitterness of the situation increased and the stress levels followed. I was actively thinking about possible solutions and how I could clean up the mess. Probably the most worrying thought was linked to explaining the situation to the people who had given me their money. For some it wasn't the first time when I lost their money, which made the situation even grimmer.

Looking for solutions consumed a lot of energy. I was tired physically, emotionally and mentally. At that point, I just wanted the situation to be over. During the past incidents, that were of a similar kind. I learnt that being sorry for myself didn't solve anything and didn't bring me any further on my path. Though at that moment it didn't matter. I was exhausted and wanted to crawl into a cave and sit there in silence feeling sorry for myself. The thought of it was appealing even though I knew it wasn't right nor fitting the character I had formed. I still decided to give it a try. Walking through the windy city at night surrounded by darkness and sleet. It all intensified the negative thoughts I had going on in my head as all those elements contributed to an image of sadness that had formed in my mind throughout the years.

Eventually my weak legs brought me to the doors of a house, at which I used to stay at the time. An old, brown house which was built after the Second World War to house veterans. Though the area was beautiful during summer, in winter it was dark and shady. Maybe it was just my perspective. I pulled my cold hands out of pockets and pushed them into a leather bag in search for keys. It took a bit to find them, under all the small items I was keeping there. Barely working hands that were numb from the freezing cold, were not contributing to it well either.

After a couple of minutes I managed to find them. I started to screw around with the lock. It was stuck so it took another minute to open the outside door. When I finally got back into the apartment, I took off all my wet clothes and walked straight into the bedroom. Laying on the couch that I considered my bed at the time. Surrounded by ambient darkness with only a small line of light that was shining through the curtains had a certain soothing effect to it. My surrounding was calm. People in the neighbouring apartments were asleep and only a few cars passed by. Even the train that usually passed every couple of hours shaking the surrounding grounds like an earthquake was not on the rails that night.

Under any other circumstances, I would have considered that night infinitely pleasant and heartwarming. The atmosphere itself reminded me of my childhood and the calm winter nights at my parent's house where my only worries were if I had anything fun to do the next day. Maybe the peaceful memories were what made that night even more dreadful than it actually was. It wasn't even about the money or the fact that once again I got fooled. It was more about the sad realisation, that so many people were so lost in their own problems that they didn't have the basic human decency or honesty. I knew that I could return all the money which was lost and that it wouldn't take much to get everything back on track. But it was eating me from the inside out that once again I was fooled because of my willingness to believe people.

I laid on my left side facing the window. Looking at the piano and the furniture that stood next to it and that small bleak of light. I sank deeper and deeper into sorrow while heavy memories flooded my headspace. I consciously decided to dedicate two hours to feeling sorry for myself. I decided that if the last time I didn't have a chance to do that than now I could see what results it could bring. I submerged myself completely into every hurting memory that I could recall. I remembered everything that had ever hurt me and what acts made me feel the most disappointed in myself. I started to imagine scenarios which I feared the most in trying to make myself cry. Crying in particular wasn't my goal. The goal of feeling sorry for myself was to let out all the emotions and sadness through crying.

Why? To release the emotional stress and pressure and to be able to look at the situation with a more sober outlook. During those two hours I tried everything I could imagine that could make me cry. Some things hurt less and others cut deep. I remember there were moments when I could feel the tears build up under my eyelids, as I tried to put myself into the most dreadful being possible. The pressured sensation started to pulsate in my eyes. A bitter taste had formed in my mouth and something was blocking my throat like a small ball of fur that a cat coughed out.

A familiar hollow feeling appeared in my chest right in the middle slightly above the Solar Plexus. As I thought I was about to shed a tear and release all the emotional pressure that had built up in me — another thought intervened. I can't recall the exact thought or the progression of it, but what I can remember is the understanding. I understood, that there were better ways to release my emotional pressure rather than force myself into a dark corner. There was a much more productive way to spend my time and it didn't involve wasting two hours on feeling like a victim. Yes it brought some kind of illusory comfort, but it wasn't true. It was temporary and fed on negative thoughts and emotions. The understanding was as bright as the sun. It didn't make me understand what I should do or how I should be, but it did tell me, what I shouldn't do and how I shouldn't do it. It was already late and there wasn't much left to do. I figured that sleep would be the most profound solution to my current situation and that maybe upon waking up, I would come up with a plan.

I woke up early, to an instant flood of thoughts and messages that lit up my screen. I didn't have much time for breakfast so a quick sandwich and a smoothie were all I scrambled up within ten minutes. While I was eating and drinking I was browsing through the messenger replying to every person who was affiliated, telling them what had happened. I was in luck as the people who were a part of the situation were mostly my close customers who have been around for a while. Their reactions were pretty calm. They knew that I was going to handle it and nobody had invested too much to worry about it right away. Besides that, most of my customers had already learnt that causing more drama from being disappointed didn't bring anything but more disappointment. The messages were sent and I was ready to head out into the snowy city. Mentally I went through a couple scenarios I had considered the night before but brushed them away as insufficient. While walking on an icy pavement. I typed a couple messages to the young man to ask him if he had any new information. By the end of writing the wind had already frozen my fingers, motivating me to put the phone away until I was somewhere warm. My go to place was a small cafe that stood by the gates to the Old Town. It was always relaxed and filled with pleasant people. Tourists and a bit more outstanding locals were always around, making the place cozy. Warm lights, sofas, ambient indie music mixed with quiet chatter. The aroma of freshly roasted coffee, soothing like a Christmas season TV commercial. The warm air hit my face like a soft wave somewhere on a beach in the Indian Ocean. I stomped my feet twice, to clean them from the snow and slit that got stuck to the bottoms and brushed off the half molten snow off of my coat. I greeted the barista and asked her if she could make me a coffee to which she nodded and turned around.

After working for the cafe for about three to four months as a social media manager. I got to meet every barista and build a nice friendly relationship with each one of them. Most of the people who worked there were really nice and kind people. Some of which were my friends. The friendly relationship and previous work experience there, made it possible for me to get free beverages long after leaving the position.

A heated sensation tickled my palms, as I rubbed them together to warm them up before unbuttoning and hanging my coat. I lifted the weight of the cold environment after which I found myself a nice place where to sit. It happened to be a blind spot by the counter. I unpacked my small notebook that I kept in my backpack at all times and found a clean page. By the time I found my pen the barista turned to me and placed my coffee on the counter. I brought it to my table while taking a small sip. At the time I drank a lot of coffee, maybe a bit too much of it. I could drink from one to twelve coffee cups a day and not feel a thing. I was aware of the unhealthy amounts that I was consuming and what consequences were to follow, so I was trying to monitor them more strictly.

The first sip I took brought a nice flavour and warmth to my senses. The cup was then placed by the notebook and I started writing. My head was fresh and I was now ready to get to the bottom of the situation. I described and deconstructed what happened last night. To figure out where I went wrong and how I could resolve it. I figured, that I opened up and let my guard down in front of a complete stranger simply because I judged people based upon myself and thought that everyone was like me and my circle. *"Fair enough."* I thought to myself. Another experience that I took for a lesson. I didn't completely understand it because as future will show, I will fall in the same trap once again. When I started to deconstruct our conversations and escalation of the events, I started to notice small hints in his behaviour and words, that I could have noticed but didn't. After a while of deconstructing I understood where I messed up and that all along the man's plan was to leave without coming back. I accepted what had happened and made a mental note about what led me to the situation.

There is a small side note I would like to make. Previously I did not include this piece of info in the story above. Besides being a trusting individual, there's another reason why I trusted the person. Because prior to the incident I had met him once and tried to do a deal with him which resulted in him disappearing for a day though the next evening he turned up and returned the money. So based on the fact that the last time he came back. I believed, that he would deliver on his promise.

Though the past couldn't be changed in a literal way. I could change some things about the current moment and I had the whole future to build and modify. I decided, that it would be the most reasonable, to find my stash of money and return the money to my customers from there. Having relaxed relations with my people and being able to continue handling the situation in peace seemed like a good idea. Then I thought to myself. How far could he go with the money that he had considering only the money that I saw hang out of his jackets pocket? He didn't have enough funds to leave the country for good. He was probably still in the city. The next thing that popped up in my head was that the city was relatively small and knowing the area in which he resided searching for him wouldn't take too much time. I evaluated a couple of scenarios in which I found him or confronted him, but neither of them seemed to be good enough to solve the situation.

My coffee was still half full. The paper cup was standing in the same location as where I had placed it after the first sip. I was done with the entry. I finished deconstructing the situation and started to pack my belongings into a backpack that was hanging off the back of the chair. A couple hours had passed and it was time to head back into action to move the situation from current state to the next one. The sun was rapidly going down, dimming the natural light. It wasn't sunset yet. A couple hours had passed since I entered the cafe. My coat was already dry and my hands felt warm and alive. I was comfortable, though I knew it was time to leave my comfort zone. When my backpack was packed and sealed, I tossed the cup into a bin and threw on my coat. Quickly buttoning it and dragging the backpack on my shoulders, I took the last breath of warm air and prepared myself to go out onto the freezing streets. I said goodbye to the barista and shut the door behind my back. Sharp wind struck my face as soon as I set my foot on the frozen stone. An uncomfortable cold moisture hit my face and slid under my clothes. I don't usually complain about the weather as I hold on to a belief that we should adopt to our surroundings and not the other way around. The weather is never *"bad"* but our clothing doesn't always fit the conditions which we're exposed to. The weather won't change if we complain, but we can evade complaining by dressing properly. Then again that day I wasn't dressed accordingly. I forgot my scarf at home and the cut of my coat was too wide to protect me from the violent wind that was raging outside. The uncomfortable feeling made me speed up my pace into a quick walk. Which we started to call *"the plug walk"*. I was no longer in the mood to be sorry for myself so I quickly made my way to the bus stop and jumped on the first bus that would take me to my apartment. When I arrived without taking my clothes off, I walked to the stash and counted out the money that I needed to return. When I was sure there was enough and that I could prevent the conflicts between me and my customers. I took off the clothes and made myself a cup of tea as a reward for at least not letting the situation spiral too far out of control. While I was brewing it I opened up the messenger and started to arrange meetings with the people to whom I owed money.

All the meetings were arranged within ten minutes. A huge weight fell off my shoulders. I felt better though not at peace. I smoke a doink sipping the cold tea that I always forget to finish before it cools down. I ordered a cab and thought through my route. That evening I was determined to once again fix what I had gotten myself into and to see after what I can do about the rest of the situation. I wanted the whole ordeal to be over. I wanted to return as much as I could though there was a subtle knowing that it won't happen. Then again, I wasn't eager for any massive actions or violent solutions. The amount of money wasn't that big, to be worth the hustle and knowing the context of the whole situation, I would end up looking stupid in both ways resolving it violently or failing at doing so. I decided to do some research as to see what I could dig up on the person and what options I had in my toolshed in general, and to see what results were within my reach.

By the next morning, I no longer owed anyone any money. It felt good. The process of waking and getting up was much more pleasant and cheerful. After finishing my casual routines I started to dig for information. It didn't take long to find out where he was living and the identities the people on which he hung out with. Just as quickly I figured that he was still in town and where he was exactly. It was now two days since the deal took place and he hasn't replied to neither of us. I decided to go to my friends and talk to them about what had happened, hoping they would have some interesting tips. When I sat down with them and told them the story in great detail. They didn't have much to say, we evaluated the violent solutions that would technically bring nothing but pain and more disappointment. The other one was to forgive and forget since the money was already gone and the backlash already eliminated.

LEARNING TO FORGIVE

When I was sitting with my friends, smoking and discussing what had gone down. I couldn't help but imagine how things would get resolved through violence. How everything got back to the original position and the person learned their lesson. The thoughts were somewhat pleasant however, not to the heart or soul. It was pleasant to the ego which was looking for revenge as it couldn't accept the fact that it was played. The mind and ego were entertained and aroused by the thoughts that they were feeding. There was also a clear, piercing understanding that those scenarios had a lot of fallacies in them and would bring the desired result but only crooked embryo of it. No matter how eager were the mind and ego to have their revenge, even they started to accept the understanding of violence not being the key to the given situation and that forgiving would be much more harmonious.

I already took a loss, I already learnt my lesson and stumbled over the rocks. How could I now forgive and forget? Wouldn't that make me a loser? Why give up and not come out as a winner? Well, maybe in the classic most common perspective that has led us so far in our history, it would be considered as a loss. Maybe not permanent but at least it would be considered a temporary loss. I left with less than I had, when I came around. Looking at it from a different perspective and coming back to what my mother had once said. *"Always be grateful when a loss is monetary, and not a loss of freedom or health"*. Money could always be made back, but health and time couldn't. When I looked beyond the financial loss that at

second view wasn't even that big, I started to see how much valuable experience I had obtained and how many new pieces of knowledge I had. I figured that it was relatively good that I had lost an amount that I did and not a much bigger one. It was also feeling good that I was cut out of that circle before I even got into it. Now I could see that the people in it weren't the type of people I would want to have in my surrounding.
Now I had a clear understanding of what people not to link myself to. Then I forgave the person. It was only a matter of his ignorance and lack of business knowledge. We could have made much more together in a long run but he decide to go for a short term gain. To me it was only a small short term loss but a long term win. So I forgave him for what he had done and the emotions he made me go through, then I did the same thing for myself and forgave myself for falling into that trap. It was no longer relevant, it was in the past and it was solved. There was no more need to feed energy to that memory or that person. I moved on.

Side note: A couple of months after the incident, when most of the memories of it already faded. I had just finished shopping and was on my way back home. When I noticed a familiar face standing on my way to the exit. The person was not alone and it took me about ten seconds to remember who it was and to my sarcastic surprise it was the person who had scammed me. When I remembered who he was I looked him straight in the the eye and smiled. When he noticed and probably remembered who I was his expressions changed in an instant to a much more shocked one. My taxi was already waiting for me and I had already moved on, so I didn't see a necessity to go out of my way and walk up to him. I just laughed and left. After that, the person became a great deal of fun and jokes for me and my friends. Seeing him there, in the exact same clothing, probably doing the same old thing. We knew that he didn't do anything incredible with the money that he had stolen.

MAPPING MY INNER SELF

The next couple of months were pretty calm and peaceful. Business went smoothly and without any major problems. There were a few miscommunications that sometimes made the progress stretch for a couple hours and there were a couple people who were busted for running their business *illegally*. In our country everything is based on the internet, taxed and monitored. They could have avoided the situation by registering their business which would secure them from the tax office while cutting their profits by twenty percent, but they decided to go for the bigger profits instead. The memory of that incident faded and everything had returned back to the course. Occasionally I remembered the scamming incidents, to go over them and refresh my memory and to be grateful for them not being around in the present moment. I was happy to be at peace and to have everything run smoothly as it was supposed to.

It was the end of January, the coldest and darkest time of the year in our region. It was almost always cloudy except those rare occasions when the sun was out for a couple minutes. Days were relatively short. About three to four hours during which, blizzards and snowstorms could be expected. I had about a half a year worth of new experiences. From a young man who was running around for essentially charity and was making small amounts of money. I had grown into a bigger businessman who made deals with various people.

Losses that once seemed big and scary were now small inconveniences that could be made back in a snap. The threats that were once frightening and brought paranoid thoughts were now just signs to be cautious and even in the worst case could be resolved. I had many connections and many sources for basically anything I could desire. I had access to countless places around the capital and the cities around it, while slowly at the same time even foreigners and businessmen from across the border started to see potential in working with me.

As my opportunities were growing, so were growing my needs and the needs of my customers. I wanted to play bigger games, and to do that I needed bigger funds and a better set of tools. Not even talking about preparation, education and precision. As my desires started to position themselves outside of my comfort zone that was no longer scary but exciting and challenging. I started to map out my desires in my headspace in order to manifest them later. For me the best tools for sorting things out have always been paper and ink. Whenever there was something which I needed to figure out. When there was something that I had to deconstruct or think through, I would always do it on paper and end up with a clear map of my thoughts. Coming from that, I've come to a place where in my awareness, I also have a sort of a catalogue of maps which are layered over each other. The map of *Souls desires*, *Emotional desires* and *Physical desires and needs*. All of them are separate and one at the same time. Being aware of them and knowing which ones to pursue at what times can be very convenient. It took me some time to come to a somewhat final conclusion. That it was time to sit down and start writing everything down. For a while, I was only contemplating doing that as I wasn't quite sure yet if I wanted to start with the changes now or in the near future. When I came to the conclusion that I indeed needed to undergo some changes in me and my surrounding In order to adopt and be practical in the new environment I got out the tools and sat down in front of a table.

I cleared the table from all the objects that weren't needed in the process. I did that to be as focused as possible and have as much free space for papers as possible. I placed three white sheets of A4 paper on the table and pulled out a blue pen. The middle piece of paper was for the desires which were coming from my soul. Those ones changed the least, so writing them down didn't take much time. I already knew that following them was the most pleasant and graceful so everything else kind of revolved around *the Souls desires*. That's why I wrote them on the middle sheet. The page with *Souls desires* was also important because the things that the soul wanted brought the truest happiness to me and the people around. Making it the primary and most pure vault of desires.

On the left side, there was a page for the *Minds desires* that were basically the career choices and things that made living and achieving *Souls desires* more pleasant and efficient. On the other side, there was a page for *Physical desires* that were things like houses, clothes, conditions and foods which made the physical life a bit more healthy and colourful. Those two pages can be also considered important, but neither of them is more important, than the other. None of them, even when combined — would be more important than the desires of the soul. Sadly people often are not even aware of what their soul desires. They consider the desires of their mind and their physical desires their primary goals and chase them without any concentrated awareness which usually leads them to disappointments. To me it didn't matter how others perceived their desires. It was clear to me that I had to have mine sorted out so I would not get lost in them and would be able to notice opportunities when they would come up and utilise them properly.

Though I use words like Souls desires and Minds desires. In general I'm referring to one's true desires that have been there for the longest. For example: Souls desires could be, to be a writer or a doctor. To help people in need or to educate children. Whatever makes your existence happy and fulfilled can be considered Souls desire. By Minds desires, I described the wishes that kind of compliment Souls desires. They make achieving them easier and more pleasant or are achieved along the way.

Physical desires are the ones that have been given to us by nature or taught by our culture, media or people around us. For example, wanting to live by the beach, have a nice car or to eat more nutritious food. Those things can be considered Physical desires.

LISTING DESIRES

I already talked a bit about the Souls/Minds desires and the Physical ones. Now let's go a bit deeper. Before we cruise into the next story. What I am about to describe can probably be called many things though I am not aware of any synonyms. It's a fairly understandable thing and you can translate it however you feel would be natural for you. The topic can be approached from a spiritual point of view, as well as a psychological one. Both of them make up the same image with just the colours being of different shades.

From a spiritual point of view I would cut the subject into three parts. *Souls desires*; *Minds desires* and *Physical desires*. All of them can be considered equally important, but at the same time the *Minds Desires* and *Physical Desires* all come from *Souls Desires* in a different shape and form.

Souls Desires: Are desires that come from the soul. Personally I considers a Souls desire, to be a desire to create, a desire to bring something good into the community or a desire to express love. Essentially the desires that warm your heart and make you happy whenever you are in the process of doing them are the desires of your soul. In my personal experience following and fulfilling Souls desires always goes well and brings more great experiences, though it may be sometimes challenging to the mind and ego.

Minds Desires: Are desires that are spawned by the conditioned mind and the ego. Some consider them to be separate and some consider them to be one. To me it doesn't really matter, so I list them both under the same category. Following them alongside the soul's desires is relatively good when you're maintaining a healthy balance. When pursuing them overpowers pursuing souls desires, it may result in confusion and dependent happiness.

Physical Desires: Can be considered the primal survival instincts. To be fed, to have shelter and a partner. They can also be the very physical manifestations of desires, like having a red car and a big house with marble floors. Those desires make the physical existence more convenient and add more shades to it. In general, the physical desires should be a mere compliment to one's big existence, but often people get lost in their physical desires and end up chasing small compliments instead of big achievements.

Being aware of my desires has always given me clarity. It made it easier for me to notice opportunities and made making decisions much easier. Knowing what I desired and when to pursue it. It was like having a to-do list attached to a map which gave me a clear overview of the items that I needed to collect and things that I had to do on my way to the final destination. Even though from time to time some desires changed and some fell off. It's always been much more pleasant to know where I'm going rather than just try to stay afloat somewhere in the middle of the ocean. Doing minor adjustments and simply keeping my eyes on surrounding environments does seem much more practical than rolling in the darkness.

From a more psychological point of view, what I'm describing is nothing more than being aware of one's nature, mind and conditions to which one has been exposed. It's much more stressful and energy consuming when one's life is incoherent. When the mind is stressed and one can't focus on what makes them happy or them alive. They start to feel more distraught and anxious. The mind's battling for its survival.

The example may seem primitive but if one's not aware of their hunger or is only partially aware of the threats that are surrounding them, the person isn't able to function properly. Some needs aren't met and stresses are present. If one is aware of them and has them sorted out at least to some extent, than arranging solutions and bringing them to fruition can be much quicker and easier.

PICKING UP THE PACE

Some progress was made. I now knew that some of my true desires were the same and some secondary desires had slightly changed by the experiences I had gone through. Interestingly enough most of my desires have been the same since early childhood. To illustrate the changes that applied to my wishes. I'd say that if in early childhood I wanted to have an apartment in New York then now I wanted to have a countryside house with a couple greenhouses. If previously I had a desire to simply have a lot of money, then later I wanted to have all the skills I'd need to be able to make any amount of money I could possibly need for any of my Physical desires.

Once again I felt the relaxing clarity in my head. The incoherent flow of thoughts, ideas and reminders of the approaching discomfort were now sorted out and placed on their shelves. The sensation of peace and understanding was magnificent. Whatever was deconstructed and rearranged on paper was now managed in the depths of my mind.
Being in the stream of pleasant euphoria. I didn't let it drag me too deep. I remembered that sorting things out is only a small fraction of work that had to be done in order to truly manifest everything which I had written down for myself. Actually, if I'm already talking about manifestation as a spiritual practice that is described in many books and lectures, I'd love to mention that I highly disagree with what many authors and *"spiritual gurus"* say. Often manifestation is described as a process when one imagines, visualises and feels as if what they desire

is already in their possession until it truly comes into physical existence. Many described it as a purely mental and spiritual practice that doesn't take any physical action and then if it's done right, everything will just magically appear. I disagree with that. It is solely my opinion and is based on my own experience. Maybe I'm nothing more than just salty because I didn't get to spawn riches and possessions out of nowhere by simply just imagining them. Maybe there are people out there who just sit in their LA mansion. Meditating spawning Rolls Royce's in their garage and it's just me who can't imagine things well enough for them to fall in front of me. Let me explain why I disagree with best-selling authors and people who gather thousands of followers around them. Well firstly I'd like to say that being able to sell something to an audience in times when literally anything can be sold for a million if a brands puts its stamp on it. And there are also many known cases of people manipulating people and profiting off of people who experienced inconveniences or traumas. My disagreement with their philosophy arises from the philosophy being too simple and one sided to be true. It sounds too easy to achieve and way too easy to abuse. Basically, without doing or giving anything, one can get anything they desire by simply putting their energy into imagining it. By imagining, one turns immortal or receives the keys to a million euro mansion. I can agree partly that imagining and visualization can aid in spotting an opportunity, or it may bring a chance to the person doing so. But seeing an opportunity is not enough for it to work out for one. In order for the opportunity to turn into something, one has to engage with the opportunity and put in their effort and energy. To bring the named opportunity to some sort of escalations. A simple desire is not enough for the world to change. As the change starts from within one and requires energy and continuous effort to truly manifest.

I didn't even notice how the time went on. The flow of it was horrid and silent. Clearly illustrating why my parents had always mentioned how time was flying. Days turned to weeks, which later turned into months. Without even noticing it I was in a relationship with a beautiful person and had an amazing crew of honest and ambitious people. My relations spread further and now I could grasp people from all over Europe and a couple of eastern countries. The work ethics were pretty much the same but improved and refined over months of trial and error, though the opportunities and services became much more complicated and serious. The opportunities were right there. Ripe and ready to be reached out to.

On one side there was a door that led to the unknown but promising that there would be a great reward. On the other side there was an infinite world of ambitions and possibilities which I could manage with ease and joy.

Oddly enough, some minor events and decisions that didn't look like much in the moment brought great relationships almost a year later. Bringing even more valuable people along. The fact that the given people appeared in my life was a blessing. The dealings had progressed into a state of a steady systematic business which due to human factor had small malfunctions every now and then. The short inconveniences didn't matter since business was once again booming. It was growing rapidly and on to the bigger scales. Though now it took relatively less effort because of the experience that had been acquired in the field. The connectivity was growing more complex, like a developing nervous system that was eager to spread and strengthen itself. Everyone worked for their own and common good as everybody understood that they were in the same boat and that the success of one was resulting in a bigger common success. Everybody was winning. It was interesting to observe so many likeminded individuals who were all a part of one big community. Those young business minded adults understood that in order to grow wealth, there was no need to take something from someone who was weaker or less intelligent. There was a common understanding that wasn't usually spoken about that explained how in order to grow bigger wealth, it would be much more practical to utilise

ones best skills in combination with the best skills of others and reaching a common goal. It wasn't spoken about much because there was no need for it. Everybody saw it in motion at all times. Whenever a deal was made or the profit was counted. There was no need to constantly talk about something that was always there, like there is no need to talk about the existence of air when it's always around.
I think it would have been more talked about if it was something that would need constant verification or acknowledgement. During that time I did quite a lot of reflecting and observing. I knew the relative seriousness of the new level and surrounding. I wanted to be sure that whatever I was doing was morally right and not a result of me lying to myself or being greedy. It was almost a year since I started, which made the whole observing and reflecting experience more impacting and emotional. I passed the same places I had passed a year ago with the same or different people. Talking about seemingly same and yet different problems and ideas. Things were always moving on without a single pause. The direction of life was always unknown and mysterious. Always leading to something new and never seen before. Yet somehow everything was similar to something that was or had happened in the past, as if everything that was in existence and outside of it moved in a never-ending cycle that changed some elements of it along the way but essentially was always the same. When the notice of cyclic nature of my surrounding became more frequent. I started to notice it everywhere which led me to a partial understanding of how different cycles worked and how the knowledge of such things could aid me in my life.

THE CYCLES OF LIFE

The idea of life being an infinite mechanism of different cycles boggled me. It was new and it made sense because I had already experienced it in various situations. The simplest example, that my mind grasped the quickest was the cycle of human life. First we are born, then we grow up and grow old while experiencing life and then the physical body dies. It has happened, is happening and will continue happen. The exact same cycle for every human being and probably most of the living organisms on our planet. While it's essentially the same thing for everyone, simultaneously it's a unique journey for every conscious being. It may have similarities to the lives of others yet is never identical. The fact that we're born and then we die wasn't mind blowing news to me. I knew it since I was a little child. Through watching movies and seeing death on the news. Death has *"already"* taken a couple of my friends and relatives and a similar fate is waiting for me and others.

The difference was in the quality of one's life. Yes the cycle was the same but what was done during the cycle and how much it was enjoyed was very different and could be chosen by the one who is living a cycle at the very moment. I started to notice how many people blindly lived their cycles. Complaining and not taking any significant action to bring a change and truly modify their cycle to make it better. As the understanding was sinking in me. I started to understand that being aware of the subject gave me more understanding about myself and more motivation to act instead of waiting. It also prompted me to discover more about my personal and universal cycles in order to interact with them in a finer way.

I don't think it's necessary to get too deep into this subject as it's too vast to talk about cycles that are hard to notice at the first glance and the smaller more common ones are too basic to waste time talking about them. If one really needs an example, imagine the four seasons of the year. All of them have their own properties and during each season, you can do some things better and others are more challenging.

During the summer it's nice to camp outside, but during winter it takes more preparation in order to not to freeze to death. If you ask me, I think it's necessary to only look into things that do or can affect one's life, and when so. The observation and action should be coming from the heart and with some precision and awareness. Looking too deep into everything and trying to find a cycle there that one could affect would be a waste of time and energy.

THE CYCLE OF MY LIFE

Observing the most important cycles of mine, which was my life. I submerged myself into observations of my own existence and the cycles, which I was a part of. The circle of my life, was the longest and most exciting cycle. That was in the field of my comprehension. Everything else came and left, changed and transformed from nonexistence to existence and from there, back to the void. With time and meditation, observing became easier. Especially after learning to focus my *"sight"* on the cycles and not minor details that triggered my emotions.

More I learnt about them, more I could see, how they affected my life and how I was able to interact with them. Some of them turned out to be completely unnecessary and were sucking out my energy. Without giving anything valuable in return. Upon understanding that I had put in effort to let go of them and replace them with something better, I noticed that some cycles didn't work as good as they possibly could. Upon deeper exploration I found out that the malfunction was coming from me. I wasn't directing my energy to it in a proper way or at the correct time. Like eating breakfast too early and getting hungry by the time you get to work. It was doing the action but not as it was designed to. Other cycles made it clear that they were very valuable, and upon better understanding could bring even more positivity and wealth into my life. Seeing all that was already motivating enough for me to start working on myself without any excuses. With time the whole practice of observing and changing myself by the environment turned into an exciting game of endless development. It didn't seem to be a burden to want to improve myself. Nothing was standing in between me and my desires. It was an exercise which benefitted me the most and foremost.

First I went over the things that laid on the surface. Relationships, visible habits, thought patterns, activities and diet. Those were the things that were the easiest to notice and change. Refining them also held great power that could stimulate much deeper changes and prompt them to happen quicker. I looked at all my surrounding relationships with a sober sight and no attachment. I evaluated them and looked at how they had cured throughout time. If I noticed a toxic relationship or one that was just floating there without any purpose. I quietly and politely ended it. Then I went over my diet as it was something that kept my physical body alive and well. Since I already had some issues with my health I didn't want to mess with it anymore. It wasn't hard to go over the food I ate, especially when I wasn't the type of person to eat different meals every day. Looking at my diet for a day gave me a review of the whole week. I noticed what foods were not good for my body and what foods seemed to be good but in reality didn't give any significant nutrients. I tried to go over my activities but it was more challenging. The things I did on a daily basis and how I acted during those things was coming from my habits and thought patterns. As I said, I tried, but that didn't result in any significant change. I couldn't skip two steps at once, while not having enough energy or *"muscle power"* to do the jump without falling down. Going over habits and thought patterns could be described as the most challenging part of changing. Habits and thought patterns came from the mind, and the mind doesn't like to change or put energy into anything that would require a lot of it. The mind started to look for excuses why habits didn't need to be changed and how the corrupt thought patterns were actually correct. It took some time, but results would follow. Upon continuous observation and remarks. The mind saw enough evidence to cooperate and change its ways. Some habits were changed and thought patterns modified according to my current being. To my surprise, my activities changed instantly as soon as some of the habits and thought patterns changed and it didn't take any effort to change my activities. They changed on their own. It wasn't only that due to a new thought pattern I suddenly didn't want to go and do something. It was more of me remembering that I was used to doing something but I simply found better things to do. Even the Universe as such, played along and rearranged my plans in a way that wouldn't include me doing things that weren't really aiding my growth and improvement.

Eventually the changes took place and grew more firm. What was once taking my focus and energy to change was now established in my being, helping me and waiting to be improved once again. All in all for some time everything was going smoothly. There were no problems and everything was going according to plan. Money was flowing in and it was about time to put some thought into how to invest or handle the funds to bring out the most of it. I don't work for money, but money is a very big part of our social existence so it's necessary to have it in order to do something and add power to it. I had seen enough people who had lost their minds from getting too much money at once or learning to make money too easily. I've seen how those people hurt themselves or lost themselves in money. Changing them into morbid shells that can still operate, but are not the same people anymore. Knowing that, I didn't want to end up like that or to be like that for any amount of time. I started to think about possible options and solutions.

CHAPTER III:
QUESTIONING MY INSTINCTS

Life wouldn't be the same without its ironic and often sarcastic humour. Like a parent that observes you, teaches you lessons and lets you learn them on your own when you get too comfortable. It is loving and at the same time it's rough and playful like an old friend. Things were going too good. In fact so great that I slowly started to grow a feeling, like something was going to strike soon. Life was too fantastic to be true and I was ready for a bitter lesson to fall on my comfortably positioned head.

For some time I could sense that something was coming, as if my insides could feel what was approaching and tensed up like they were preparing for a blow. For a while I lived with that feeling. Dormant and hoping that the feeling would pass with the potential danger. I tried to be careful and attentive and not get into stupid ordeals which would result in losses. Around that time I also started practicing with my intuition. Relying on my senses became more relevant than ever before. Though in the past I had some experiences when my intuition had guided me to the right place or safely took me off track in order to avoid a conflicting situation. Those experiences were far in the past and weren't easy to remember. Even remembering them didn't have much value as the past experiences were hard to translate into the present moment. I'm simply saying I didn't have any certain sensation to rely on that would tell me what was relatively right and wrong for me. I decided to be more attentive. Not having anything to relate to wasn't a reason to abandon something that held great potential in it. It was my closest and truest guide. Feeling that it was something I had to develop and knowing that the previous experience didn't have much use. I understood that I had to pay extra attention to the processes that were going on the inside of me and how they responded to what was going on in the surrounding.

I was as attentive as my capacity allowed me to be. I tried to see more in everything that resonated with me and tried to track every sensation that arose within. Meanwhile, I was also pondering a desire to legitimise my business. Indeed I was exposing it to taxes but simultaneously I was making it easier and more transparent. Besides, it would let me collect profits much easier and in case of any problems I could release the lawyers. I thought it was a good idea and that it wouldn't take too much. The next of couple days I spent researching local business laws and what would it take to open a legal business. I figured that with knowing my capabilities, should I find an investor, I could reach much higher right away. Maybe you're already seeing it. I was looking for an easy way, which often results in a tough lesson. Meeting a couple of wealthy people only brought me more questions than answers. I had to learn more in order to start my business. A desire for an investor rose even more than before. The more questions I answered, the clearer it became that an investor would be necessary and would make the whole business plan work out much quicker. The sensation of something being off was still there. It was there long enough for me to get slightly used to it and it was no longer in the middle of my awareness stressing me out. It was now subtly humming in the back of my heart. The thought of legitimising my business was becoming more and more interesting, as by my calculations and thoughts it could rid me of many obstacles that I had ran into. I understood, that there would be new obstacles that would come along my path, but I was more optimistic to meet those new barriers and get over them rather than get bamboozled every now and then. The active search for an investor didn't go too well. I started to accept the idea that if I wanted to have a successful business and have it completely legal. I would have to build it up all by myself. At least in the beginning. The idea was brewing in my head. I was slowly gathering pieces of info which would lead me to my desired destination.

One seemingly regular day I was going around town minding my business. Nothing special happened that day and nothing was supposed to go down either. I was sitting in a cafe drinking coffee while a thought about calling it the day was circling on my mind. It was pretty early, around six in the evening. I contemplated going to the store and then heading home when a message interrupted the process. It was my friend. She wanted to meet and go out for a cup of something hot. As I enjoyed drinking coffees and I hadn't seen her in a while I thought it wouldn't be too bad if I had another cup while catching up with her. She said that she was driving a car and that she could pick me up. That sounded great considering the weather, so I kindly agreed to which she offered a location where we'd meet. About ten to fifteen minutes passed and my phone vibrated again. The most recent notification had a small writing on it, saying *"I'm here."* to which I quickly got up. I'm not a car specialist but I could remember the shape and color of her car. When I made it to the location that we agreed upon, I tried to spot her vehicle which surprisingly wasn't there. I stood there for about a minute thinking that maybe she knew that I was going to exit as soon as she would say she was there so maybe she wasn't completely there yet?
When I finished that thought I noticed a door of a grey car open. A wrist with a couple rings on fingers sprung up and waved. Knowing that I wasn't acquainted with many people who wore rings there weren't many possibilities of who it could be so I set my steps towards the grey car. I opened the door and sat in the backseat. To my surprise in the driver's seat there was a man who looked much older than my friend was. I greeted both of them and we started to move. The ride wasn't the most comfortable as the presence of that man did not feel

pleasant. Not that I felt intimidated or in danger. It felt like something was telling me that the man sitting in front of me wasn't a man who would be trustworthy or bring much good. Those thoughts were present during that time. By the time I'm writing this, I can say that the sensation I got was telling me that the person sitting in front of me was full of shit.

They asked me if I knew any good cafes which would have good beverages and a nice atmosphere to which I laughed and gave them the address. As we drove the driver played some metal music from the speakers and emotionally drummed along on the steering wheel. That sight surprised me even more. I've known Carmen for several years and I've never seen her listen to that type of music. Not that I have anything against it. I faked enjoying the music choice so I wouldn't create even bigger discomfort for me and my fellow citizens in the car. Occasionally we engaged in small conversations about each other that sounded more like interrogations. Something that I noticed right away was that whenever he spoke about some-thing he tended to glorify himself while adding bizarre details that weren't too outlandish to seem obviously false, but extremely complimentary to his side of the story. Maybe he's just egoistic and that's all. When we arrived at the café to drink there we decided instead to order them for takeaway and drink them in their new apartment. My friend was very excited to show me her new place of living that she was renting with her new man. The difference in their age seemed very bizarre to me, knowing that he was about thirteen years older than her. Well, maybe she's tired of young men and is looking for somebody with more experience? I decided to brush off that thought and accept whatever there was. After all, she was my friend and I knew how her previous relationship went, so seeing her with somebody older wasn't really that surprising.

We pulled up to their driveway. It was a colourful street filled with cozy private houses and apartment buildings that were built about seventy years ago. The whole block was covered in a thin layer of snow. With the orange streetlights, it had its own urban beauty. The driver came out of the car first and lit up a cigarette, marking that we would have to stand outside for a couple more minutes until he finished his smoke. During that time we again had some small talk and a few laughs here and there. After he flicked away the butt his hand reached for the keys after which he unlocked the outside door.

The corridor was wooden and almost as cold as the space outside of the house. The smell that was present in that staircase was the same smell that I have sensed in all soviet time buildings, as well as my great grandparents summerhouse. Whenever I entered a building that had this particular smell it always threw me back into the times when I was about five years old. Staying the summer at my great grandparents' house. It had its own charm and nostalgia to it. At its most, it birthed a bit of curiosity about what elements caused that smell to appear. My guess was that it was dust, old wood and paint that stood stale for decades.

When I was a child, starting from about four years. My parents used to work a lot. Especially my father who was working from nine in the morning up until three in the morning. Of course, my mother was a hard working woman as well who was often attending many meetings with her customers. Not to mislead anyone, my parents did spent time with me and the time that we spent was amazing and educating all at once. Yet as my parents were smart people, they knew that if they wanted to provide for me and give me what they considered important they had to maintain their jobs. We lived close to my grandparents. I was often brought to their house to stay the night or just hang out there until one of my parents was able to pick me up and bring me home. My grandparents lived close to my home at the time as well as the kindergarten that I attended and the school to which I went a couple years later. Though their apartment was rather small and humid, even so during summer. I was sent to my great grandparent's summerhouse. There I spent an enormous amount of time in the woods. The forest was big and had a couple homes and summer houses around it. I was always trusted to go out alone as I knew my way back and if I got lost, somehow I'd end up

We went to the second floor. Each step squeaked and rattled whenever he put his weight on it. It sounded as if the stairs were about to crumble. I thought it was funny but out of respect I kept the giggles to myself. The squeaky stairs are a reoccurring theme in Soviet time houses and as I've been to many I expected a Soviet time apartment to be behind the door as well. He turned the key and a click was heard. The door unlocked and he entered to the other side. As I stepped in I was quickly instructed to leave my snowy shoes by the door so I wouldn't make the floor dirty. An oddly straight forward and a bit rude thing to say, but whatever. For the short period of time that I had known him I already had a relatively big collection of weird mental notes that I had made about him. Glorifying himself, belittling others and being extremely rude were only few things that were on the surface. When I got my shoes and coat off I finally set my eyes on the apartment and got to get a good look at it. The apartment had a spacious living room with a big couch and a sofa. On my right there was a nice small fireplace that looked very convenient considering the weather outside. Carmen offered me a cup of tea and we sat down. They laid on the couch and I sat on the sofa. As we drank tea and rolled doinks, our conversations started to take shape. Discussions took a turn towards business and Artur's started bragging about the businesses in which he had invested and how his other businesses were working out well. Again I heard a lot of glorying but what I saw was somehow backing him up. I couldn't argue with him while sitting in his home. Especially when I had no clue who he really was. He was trying hard to leave an impression of a serious man who had a wide reach but something was bugging me. To me, there were too many signs that resonated with me in a weird way. As if my senses could feel that something was wrong but couldn't pinpoint what was the source of the disturbance. I decided to be simply aware of the responses that my body gave.

The conversation went on and now we had a live discussion about my business idea and how it magically went along with his business plan too, that he came to realize in our town. Describing my idea in detail carried me away. I was no longer talking about it in an objective way but was describing how I dreamt of my business to bloom. Being submerged in my daydream I forgot about the signals that my body was giving me. For a moment I remember how I thought to myself *"I can't believe that our ideas are matching. It must be a sign from the universe."* While it was a type of a sign from the universe, it wasn't the sign I was eager to see. I completely ignored the lesson that was being taught to me. Soon I will get to the lesson that it was teaching me as in the end it will make sense to me and therefore to you as well. At that moment though, the lesson that I was learning was placed in the background while a completely new situation emerged.

It was getting late by now and at that point I had to make a decision. We either agreed on carrying on with planning that would extend our relations, or I would pack my things and head home. The look on my friend told me that I should stay for longer as the conversation could possibly birth something. My mind as well had noticed how the conversation was evolving and that apparently the man was trying to see if I was going to make a decision. I offered him to meet the next day and see if we could do something with our mutual idea. As I finished the sentence a grin arose on his face and his eyes changed. As if he snapped out of a bubble and was now completely focused on me. He said that he was glad I had said that because if I didn't, he would want me to leave instantly. That made me feel weird. Something told me that I had made a wrong decision while something else was telling me that I made a great decision. After arranging a meeting for the following evening, the tone of our conversation changed. It was friendlier and the topics got more casual. We had a couple more doinks and tea to which I started to feel tired. It was already late and my body was yearning for sleep.

As I took the last drag, I started to nudge my body to get up and prepared myself for the road. While packing my bag I called the cab to pick me up. I left the apartment feeling uneasy. In a way the uneasiness can be translated into excitement over a possibility to turn my plans into reality while at the same time a sensation of the whole scenario being too easy to be true was ringing in the back of my skull. The same uneasy feeling haunted me until the moment I sat down on the same sofa in front of him, talking about my idea and proposing to unite our forces for a common interest. Our tones and the sentences that we spoke were of the same context and nature yet our intentions and interests were completely different.

MUDDY WATERS

Even though I tied myself with that person verbally no legal ties were done. For a while I analysed and contemplated Artur's. I tried to figure what were his intentions and why was he with my friend? A couple thoughts arose and painted some images describing gold digging or an older man using a young and naive girl for whatever reasons he had in mind. Scenarios were unpleasant and seemed as if I was judging them for some or no reason at all. That made me brush off the pictures and simply carry on. I thought that it was unfair from me, to look at them in such light and go over judgmental thoughts regarding them. It felt true but the truth was not pleasant and I didn't want it to be what it actually was. What seemed obvious to my heart was too dirty for my mind, which was trying to follow the heart. I put those speculations aside and looked beyond them. The whole time that I was about to spend with them, I closed my eyes on every weird thing I noticed, subconsciously quieting down the intuition, that I was trying to develop so hard. An oxymoron situation where I was going against a desire that I was so excited to bloom. Back then I didn't know any better so I went along meeting him almost daily. Talking and planning our business. Not even being aware of it, I was helping him prepare a solid scheme to fool me and make me give him money.

Our meetings became a daily routine. We either drove around in his car that had changed after our first meeting to a black Lexus, or we sat in my kitchen drinking tea and writing down our business plans. Another reason why I couldn't call it a scam right away was because we actually followed through on most of the steps that were planned in the beginning. He had also taught me quite a couple valuable lessons and insights about some elements of the business world and some specific professions. When we were not cruising around or sitting at each other's apartments, he sometimes took me out to meet some other people he was affiliated with.

During those meetings my attention and awareness were peaking. I paid attention to every emotion that surfaced on faces of people and how the environment changed. An enormous amount of attention was given to names and contacts of people who we were meeting. Something was clearly telling me that at some point I was going to need them. Even though he always mentioned me as an unimportant observant, I went out of my way to make some small conversations with the people he took me to meet so they would have some sort of trust for me. As our plan was progressing, I was growing more trust for Arturs and gave less attention to the sketchy feeling I had about him. Eventually we went to see a landlord for the place we wanted to rent for our business. The speech he gave to the business woman and the lady who owned the space was impressive. Every sentence he said sounded firm and certain: As if there was no doubt in his honesty. Nothing stood out in a weird way. To our pleasure, the ladies believed him just as much as I did. The next step was to get the business legalised and my name engraved in it. We spent a couple days planning a visit to a lawyer that would later help me sign papers that would bond me to a temporary debt that I picked up due to my lightheartedness. Arturs paid for the lawyer's services and the company was mine.

Maybe I mentioned it before, but it was my first experience with getting into legal business as somebody who owned and managed a company. There were many things I didn't know about or didn't know what the things I should have looked out for were. While having multiple experiences with being scammed and with countless encounters with seeing people and businesses getting scammed. I was aware of a possibility of such thing happening to me. Being fooled by fake kindness and excitement of following my desires. I never even thought about checking Arturs background or even googling his name, thus playing along to the deception that was taking place around me. I have to mention that there always were warning signs posted around him, telling me to pay attention and possibly distance myself from the whole situation.

But by that time my eyes were covered enough to answer every assumption with a lie that was provided to me previously.

I ate every lie like a cookie. At that point not even questioning what was inside of it or why it was given to me. I thought that the universe was being kind to me and was finally handing me what I had desired for some time. Instead it was in the process of teaching me to trust my intuition and to not let myself get carried away by words of people who mean no good. Throughout my whole experience with Arturs, I never understood why he had a weird smirk on his face and why all the people who he called his long term partners and friends knew him only for a short period of time. Small warning signs that I never questioned enough as there was no serious motive to it. I didn't lose anything yet and the stress I was feeling felt like it was from the effort that I was putting into changing my lifestyle for the better.

So far the business was registered on my name. The plan was to split it as soon as he provided the investment money he was talking about. He claimed that he was an important figure in a big foreign investment company and a part of some other smaller businesses locally. He showed me some websites and pictures of things that to an unexperienced person looked like solid proof. Later I discovered that even experienced people had a hard time figuring out who he was as the false image that he had created around himself was so elaborate and thought through for years in advance. Not saying that he was planning the scam for years but that he had composed the image and all the evidence years ago and was using the tools he had in many places and on many unsuspecting people. To add even more, later I found out that Arturs was a somewhat famous in some regions for his skilled and arrogant scams.

We now had the legal paperwork and we were ready to start our business. It was about time we found a space to settle our items and start buying in the products for sale.

At that time, I didn't have too much money and he had a bit more than I did. Knowing what car he drove and the apartment he lived in.

(Plus taking into consideration the story that he told me about having multiple kids from different women and having to support them.)

The money he had promised to invest was in the vault of his investment company or in the hand of people who we together would need to assist in order to get the money from them. To me it didn't seem weird at all. I was young and trying to start a properly working business with a help of an investor. I expected that it would take time to get an approval or something to receive the investment. On another note, I didn't consider it weird to help him make money with his other businesses so he could support mine. Like my natives say *"A hand washes the other hand."* During the time of our communication Arturs told me about his alleged businesses. How some of them were abroad and how some were local but very low profile. The so called proof he showed me was convincing enough and I didn't feel like creating conflicts by questioning his honesty. I already learnt that to him the image he was projecting alongside his pride were crucially important to him and having any doubts about them would be an enormous insult to him. I was too neutral to start conflicts or even waste my energy on thoughts about that and was too interested in getting the money he was talking about to create a cloud of doubt around his idea of investing.

When it was time to get the money for our business, he showed me some drafts of letters that he was about to send to his fellow chairmen to request the funds. The email he was sending the final message from had an extension of the business he was claiming to be a part of, so again I didn't question the validity. He said that it was going to take time and if we wanted to start up our business quicker, we would need to put in a bit more than just writing a letter. He flashed a couple hundreds and said that the cash I just saw was going to go into his businesses so he could multiply it and get more.

He looked at me with a decisive expression and asked if I wanted to contribute to raising money for the business I was so eager to build. Obviously implying that I as well should put in some cash, so I gave him some money. I've heard a saying *"Money didn't like to be stale."* Speculating that all sayings have a true origin I held on to it. From that point on, a month long journey into exhaustion, realisations and feeding a leech started.

Telling this story, I've probably made quite a fool out of myself. At that point I didn't know it yet, but when I found out. I felt rather stupid and demoralised for a week or two. Not to even mention that the realization to which I was coming for a month wasn't like a snap or a sudden awakening. It was a stressful continuous effort of digging out the truth and dragging it to the surface.

Mostly it was minor things. Some gas money for driving me around. Borrowing my computer and never returning it. Then some more money for projects and deals that never got to fruition and just stayed somewhere behind the border of my knowledge. After noticing a pattern of failing deals and inconveniences which were arising on his side. I started to grow more and more suspicious. The speculations that were now coming to my head were not that easy to brush off. Taking into notice how it was affecting my wallet I wasn't planning to ditch those thoughts. In case you're wondering, the reason why I didn't quit as soon as I didn't get my computer back or a couple of his plans failed was simply because I never had a mentality of a quitter. If I started something I was determined to finish it, especially when it was something as big as my desire or a goal I wanted to achieve. The tone that we had during our conversations sounded as if we always battled for dominance in which we did. Even though I saw how his businesses were failing, my balls were too big to call quits and leave him at that. I wanted to prove to myself and get the thing out of a ditch. In the rush of starting our business and slightly phased by all the obstacles that we had faced so far, I was eager to get us back on track.

He used the chance to take some devices and services on my business either without my knowledge or by tricking me into thinking that those things were crucial for success. Around that time he started to be less present, claiming he was abroad managing his businesses and collecting money for ours. He was somewhere beyond my vision but what was still in my reach was all the failure I had witnessed as well as the consequences of his actions that started to build up on my shoulders. Seemingly he was dealing with things to solve our mutual and his personal problems. For some reason, every failure and attempt hit me instead. Eventually my friend and his girlfriend started to be more present around me than him and that later started to lead us to a door which would shows the unpleasant discovery that was the truth behind it all.

TRYING THE DOOR

Disappointments and failures became more frequent and so became my thoughts about him not being who he claimed he was. My trust in him was evaporating quickly, like water that was thrown on hot stones. I wasn't furious or angry. I was simply curious to figure out what was going on and as the stress level was rising, so did my desire to distance myself from his persona.

More bad news came in and more questions arose. I and other people who were involved in deals with him that were put on hold due to a lack of finances. Everybody wanted to know where he was and when were they getting paid for their services. I wanted to know the answers just as much as the others because I wanted to give them some clarity and have all the pressure grounded. In general I didn't mind stressful situations and things not going as planned as according to my philosophy, it's a completely natural occurrence. The thing is, that it's no longer natural when a stressful situation stretches out for over a month and involves many people, who are even more confused than you are. After many attempts to reach him over different messenger apps and many numbers that he had. None of them were successful. I decided that I would no longer wait for him and start to resolve things on my own. If I did that, I would rid myself of stress and when he came back we would get our personal things resolved. One casual evening as I was sitting in the kitchen. I was reading some articles on the internet, accompanying the activity with a drink and a cup of tea. It was dark outside and the frequency of bypassing cars was rapidly dropping. I was midway through a paragraph when a sharp bell ring made my neck go tense. The unexpected noise startled me. I looked to my left and on my screen, there was a small bubble that said *"New Message Received."* I slid my finger across the screen, unlocking the device and brought the app to the foreground. The only chat that had a notification bubble next to it was Arturs girlfriend Carmen. She was asking if I had any info and if I was able to come over for a chat. That late evening I had nothing better to do and my morals were giving me hints that I should go. At the very least I could help her cope with what was possibly going on. I informed her that after a short while I was going to call a taxi and come over. After finishing the processes that were interrupted by the messaging, I once again reached out for my phone, to call a cab. When a driver confirmed that he was going to pick me up. I packed some of my belongings and got myself dressed.

At that time there was no more traffic so the driver arrived in about three to four minutes. Quickly hopping over a pile of snow and making a couple risky slippery steps towards the car I opened the door and jumped in. After greeting the driver I told him the address of our destination and put on my headphones. At first, I intended to play some music to get my thoughts off of what was about to drain me of all my remaining energy. Sabotaging myself, I got carried away thinking about what she may ask and what was I going to tell her. The thoughts consumed me from head to toe and I forgot to turn on the music. The whole way there I sat in silence, running through possible scenarios of how our conversation may go and what would be my replies to all the possible questions she could ask. While a part of me was actively trying to control the damage that was being caused, another part of me was only speculating and guessing what could possibly be behind all of this exhausting hustle. I barely noticed it at first, but the driver smoothly stopped the car and looked me in the eyes through his mirror. Though there was no music playing, I took off my earphones, to let the driver know that I was listening to him. During the same moment with a corner of my right eye, I noticed a greenish tone plastered all over the wall. We arrived. I paid the fee which appeared on drivers tablet, thanked him for a pleasant ride and left the car. I messaged Carmen as soon as I came out to notify her of my arrival and make extra sure that she would open the door quickly. Freezing outside wasn't something I wanted to add to an already messed up situation. A slight hum reached my ears, the magnetic lock was disabled. For a second it was hilarious that such and old wooden door that couldn't even hold the heat inside was secured with a modern magnetic lock. The fun lasted for about a second after which I pushed the door as hard as I could and ran into the building. Once again, I walked up the squeaky stairs accompanied by the previously mentioned Soviet smell. The door to her apartment was already open and a light stream of heat was coming through the breach. I walked in and closed the door behind my back. There was no *"man"* in the house so I didn't bother rushing my shoes off. Carmen walked out of the kitchen and we greeted each other with a hug. I decided it was time to take off my shoes and put my coat in the closet. While I was removing the top layer of my clothing, we exchanged a couple sentences asking each other about how our days went and how each one was feeling. After that, she again offered me tea. As a person who will always accept a cup or a pot of tea at any time of the day, the offer was accepted without any hesitation.

A hot cup was standing on a left handle of the same sofa I sat on when I entered this apartment for the first time. On the same low couch that was in front of me she sat exactly like that first evening. The heat from the beverage was strong and was slightly burning my palm though I didn't dare to let it go. The handle was too soft and the cup could easily fall over and ruin the sofa. Burning my mouth and tongue like an amateur wasn't a part of my plan either so I put the cup on the floor. I got out my pouch to roll a small doink to smoothened the lengthily discussion that was about to begin.

I've known Carmen for over a year. A kind light hearted person who was slightly naive, but very lovable for her friendly persona and motivated attitude. When we just met, she had many friends and many more people knew her. She was outgoing and liked to work in places that had many people visiting. She was responsible at work and great with people, making it a great combo for receiving many tips. When she met her new boyfriend, he manipulated her into lying to most of her friends and borrowing money from them, after which he instructed her to cut them off. He explained by saying, that they were fake or not serious enough to spend time with. As a result she had blindly ruined many nice relationships, leaving her alone with all the problems that he put on her shoulders. Our friendship was always uplifting and light. Most of the mutual experiences we held were creative and of a kind nature. That evening I could feel a whole banquet of emotions   which were spawned by the new set of experiences that we attained. Ever since he came around our friendship turned from creating, to solving problems and trying to help each other figure out what was going on and how to deal with it. It was acceptable, but not the most pleasant scenario to follow. There were many more positive things we could have and wanted to talk about but all of them had to be put aside, as they weren't as prioritised as the topics that were bothering us.

In her eyes I could see disappointment, sadness, exhaustion, confusion and some small sparks of anger. I knew that she didn't want to talk about things that she invited me to talk about. It was clear as day that she had a hard time coping with what was going on and even harder time with wrapping her head around every bill that he had posted on her name. I think what hit her the hardest wasn't the sudden heartbreak or a realisation that Arturs didn't truly love her or wanted to have her as his last love. What delivered the most devastating blow was the fact that an older man who posed as an experienced, rigorous man and promised her the whole world and his heart, had simply used her for monetary and emotional gain.

I rolled my doink in silence, glancing at her from time to time to see the emotions that were currently on her face. At the same time in my own head I was trying to recollect my thoughts and compose proper sentences to deliver some sort of a message without misleading her.

The doink was rolled into a sharp slim cone that was about nine centimeters long. After lighting it up I took the first hit and turned my face to Carmen. It was time to start our discussion. Before I was going to talk I wanted to know what she already knew. What was going on for her and what she was dealing with to save both of us from additional confusion and potential info that could distress her even more. *"Any updates?"* was what came out of my mouth and turned to be the opening line for our conversation. She said *"No. He hasn't replied in days."* *"What a weird relationship."* I thought to myself, as I evaluated the fact that he's been occasionally sending me messages in attempts to ensure me that everything was going to be alright. Along the way he had also asked me to hide information from Carmen and keep her occupied with lies so she wouldn't stress him. When he asked me that I told him that I would help him, but I didn't keep my word as it would have been an insult to my friendship with his so called girlfriend. I told her that he's been talking to me from time to time and explained to her what the topics we discussed were. It was interesting to see how much he was lying to her and to me and how different were the lies even though he knew that we were good friends. That was probably the first breach in his plan that then led to his exposure. After a short recap the expression on her face became more worried than angry and the tone of her voice became more tense and disrupted. She said that their landlord had called her. The landlord was unhappy that they still hadn't paid their bills for the month that just passed and that they didn't pay their debts from the month before. The news baffled her. She had already enough stress on her shoulders and now that?! Arturs convinced her that he paid all the bills and that there was nothing to worry about.

He even showed her a bank transfer receipt so there was no base for her to think something was off. She added when she asked the landlord about the transfer. His reply was that he as well received the receipt through email from Arturs but the money never came through. The last bit of excuse she had to offer was to say that her boyfriend had a foreign bank account meaning the transfers may take up to three business days. That also didn't work as landlord quickly interrupted her by saying that it's been far more than three days. In the storm of bad news that was the toughest blow that hit her. The landlord told her he was coming for a visit with a colleague and insisted that it would be great if Arturs was around too.
I asked her if there was anything else going on in her life that was related to her man.

There was a small silence which was followed with a sigh. A few seconds later she took a breath and quietly started to talk. When their relationship was still fresh and unstained, they had a plan to build a business. To do that just like me she needed money. She didn't have a stable source of income because of her boyfriend demanded that his woman must not work regular jobs. Due to that the only way for her to attain any money was to ask for loans from her friends and family. As that was her primary option she went to all of her good friends and asked them for money. The ones who refused to give her money and expressed their mistrust for Arturs were met with a salty stare. The ones that did give her money because of not knowing the reason or nature of the situation were appreciated. The kind friends who she once thanked were now feeling mistreated, as she wasn't able to return them the money she promised and by being defensive caused even more drama. If that wasn't bad enough, in the pursuit of emotions and excitement Arturs offered her to take a loan from a bank or even better, multiple banks so she could start her business off quicker.
As he claimed to have a lot of business experience, she didn't even consider that under some circumstances she wouldn't be able to return the money and would fall into a pit of debts.

The situation that I was now picturing was pretty unpleasant. A few other grim strokes of paint were torn onto the image when I heard her saying that he had persuaded her into selling her car and giving him all the earnings. I asked her: *"What did he do with all the money?"* To which she just lifted her shoulders. The evening was eventful to say the least. I thought for a second if I wanted to know any more about her situation. The curiosity in me tingled and I asked if there was anything else that I should be aware of? The last bit was like a juicy cherry on top of a cake, beautifully illustrating the expensive taste of our freeloader. Between all the activities that were packed into their busy day. He found a spare hour to take her into a couple shops and took a couple phones on her name which she never saw after the initial purchase. Every single valuable item, every last cent. He took everything, even her bank card which he casually used to pay for his meals and gas while being in the neighboring countries. The situation was so bad and unreal that it was almost surreal and comedic. Like a comedy/drama movie shot by a group of stones who thought it would be funny to make every possible circumstance go against the protagonists. Looking at the ongoing situation with humoring thoughts was the only way to dilute the bitterness at hand.

I took my last drag and pushed the roach face down into the ashtray, dragging it along the surface to distinguish the leftover coal. The smoke stopped. Marking that it was time for me to start packing. I slowly got up and gathered the items that were scattered between the kitchen and living room. It took me about ten minutes to get all my things together, get dressed and say goodbye. About the same time as it took the driver to arrive to the location. After leaving her house, I no longer thought about the whole situation. Thinking about it had already exhausted me and there was no need to continue doing so, as there was nothing more to bring out of it.

OPENING THE DOOR

I woke up feeling refreshed and full of motivation. I didn't know exactly where that feeling was coming from but it was something I felt I had to use to its full potential. The fresh headspace allowed me to zoom out of the situation I was focused on and I could see the bigger picture. I understood that dwelling on the same things didn't help and just worrying and venting over drama only brought more stress. Something clicked, I had to route my energy into other places to see what outcomes those could bring. Counting up my losses and going over a thought about how much time I had wasted didn't bring any valid solutions. While I was doing just that I had completely forgotten about all the other options I had in my possession. I forgot that there were many more sources of solutions in my surrounding than reasons to not pursue them. The next step was to figure out the sequence of actions that could lead me out of the mess that I had dragged myself into while not letting myself sink any deeper. But how could I make sure I wouldn't fall into any other traps?

While making breakfast I scribbled a draft of a To-Do list on a sheet of paper to have a better overview of steps that could potentially fix small bits of chaos in different areas that in the end would result in the overall misbalance being brought back to proper function. Suddenly I remembered how I was trying to develop my intuition and how I was frustrated about not being able to hear it. One thought led to another and the next thing I knew, I was pondering the events in a light that made everything look like a lesson on what didn't feel good, so later I would know what not to go for and what feelings to seek.

Once again I had encountered the somewhat ironic aspect of life. Previously I mentioned how life was like a person and liked sarcastic pranks. Playful and loving spirit of life had once again played me. To me as a self-centered human being, it felt bitter to be pushed out of balance by life. At the same time it taught me the lesson I was so eager to learn.

As a somewhat lazy specie, I didn't want to attend classes but wanted to know the subject thoroughly and master the craft. Life doesn't work like that. To know my comfort and capacity, I had to feel the hot and the cold on my own skin.

A quiet hissing sound was present in the background until it grew louder and started boiling. A sharp click bounced against my eardrum alerting, that the water was ready to be poured into a cup. I brewed myself some tea while new questions slowly started to sprout in my mind. After finding my balance and comfort on a wooden chair I placed a piece of paper and a pen in front of me and opened my mind to any new thoughts. The tools laying in front of me were there to provide an ability to make quick notes in case an especially bright idea happened to hit me. I didn't want to let anything valuable slip.

I sat there for a while, thinking about what questions I wanted to find answers to. Previously, I was asking the same questions. I was looking in the same places and expected new answers to magically appear. Writing down every question that popped up in my head wasn't a good idea since either would be a waste of paper and energy and would result in having a bunch of questions asking the same thing.

ASKING THE RIGHT QUESTIONS

As much as I can recollect I started asking questions since early childhood. When I was with my grandma I asked her all the questions that could come to my mind. It didn't matter if it was something practical or just asking why was the sky blue. The context didn't matter and it wasn't of any importance if it was my first or sixth time asking it. She would always answer. Getting answers was easy, therefore I didn't put much energy into thinking or composing the questions properly. When it came to my dad, at first I didn't get to spend much time with him so I had more time to think about the questions I wanted to ask before he left for work. I can remember how from time to time he told me not to ask stupid questions. That happened when I asked something too simple or something that didn't have a meaningful answer.

When I grew older, I started to face bigger challenges and questions became more complex. It became more important to build my questions correctly so the answers that I would receive would be clear and precise. In retrospect, if I had asked the right questions. Many events would have gone much smoother and without the unnecessary extra hustle. In other cases, when my awareness was wide enough, I managed to ask questions which made my task clearer and the progress easier.

Another interesting memory that keeps coming back to me is of when I was at my parent's house a couple years ago. It was pretty late and most of my family was asleep. My dad and I were the only ones who were still awake because he was reading something and my head was filled with worries that didn't let me sleep in peace. As the time passed on I vented over my drama without finding any solutions that would satisfy the mind. After a while I decided to go downstairs and ask my dad for advice. Knowing that he was more experienced and obviously smarter than me, I thought turning to him would ease my search for a solution and be a sort of a shortcut to my goal. I went downstairs and sat next to him. He noticed that I was still awake and put away a booklet that he was reading at the time. He asked me why was I still awake? To which I started to explain the situation I was in. It was nothing serious or superficial but to a young mind like mine, even a small surface problem seemed big and somewhat frightening. Though the issue was minor, the worrying that I had done had blown my idea of the problem completely out of proportion.

We sat there for a while. He was listening quietly and carefully, as I was extensively describing what was bothering my peace. When I was done explaining, I asked him about what should I do. After going over the problem one more time, I thought now was the time to receive the salvation I've been waiting for. Instead I got a moment of silence and a sigh that was followed by a suggestion to repeat the story and what the problem was. I thought he didn't understand me and started to tell the story again. After another monologue, he still didn't give me any solutions but offered me to think out loud. How would I solve the situation?

At first, I told him that I didn't know. After all, that's why I came to him. To that he replied that I did know the answer but was too lazy to figure it out myself. I didn't have a good comeback so I agreed and started to vocalise my ideas. When I started listing them I stared to turn down as soon as I named them, and others I cut off on a half a sentence as I understood that they wouldn't work out. A feeling of agitation started to rise in me. My heart rate increased and not being able to come up with a solution started to annoy me. I started listing the next one and between two words I stuttered as something in my head clicked again. The weight of drama that was hovering over me fell down and dissolved at my feet. I knew what could get the problem solved. A smile stretched across my face and a warm feeling of joy washed over me. I thanked him to which he responded with a smiled. After that I went back upstairs. I was glad by the results and fell asleep in peace.

WALKING IN THE ABYSS

Next couple days were full of constant activity and damage control. My waking time was divided into two sectors. Communicating with the people involved in the situation, paying them back my debts and handling new deals to make some money. Thanks to my great circle, the finances were being recovered in a promising pace. After a couple nights I could already pay back most of my debts and could see myself getting a new computer. The goal was now clear. It was no longer relevant if the man was going to return and fix everything, or never come back at all.

The benevolent inner child deep inside of me, still had a grain of faith for him. Hoping that when he returned he would tell me an exciting story about why everything took so long and would carry out everything he's been promising.

The crucial questions that desperately needed to be formed and answered were now taking shape, after which I could already somewhat see the outlines of opportunities that could help me resolve all the imbalance. I knew what I had to do to clear my name from any debts and unpleasant vibrations, as well as regain my financial comfort to carry on doing things I love the most. Deep inside, I've been feeling that I should let go of the man and no longer keep my mind occupied with thoughts about what and why it happened. Something within me knew that whatever he was doing was not worth thinking about and that if it already happened it was meant to happen. I shouldn't try too hard to retrieve the things from him. On the other hand my mind and ego were feeling mistreated and to an extent annoyed by the arrogance of that man who had bamboozled me sitting in my kitchen, drinking the tea I made for him. We judge people based on ourselves, so to my mind it was incomprehensible that a person could sit in someone's home, accepting all of their kind offers and then, scams them and a bunch of other people like it's nothing. It took some time for the mind to come to terms with the fact that some people don't have the same morals as I and it started to cool down. Eventually I lost the emotional attachment to the situation and it started to bother me less. Talking to the victims of the unfortunate events and re-growing my financial balance took some time and energy, but even as I was accepting what had happened. I still wanted to dig out all the truths and uncover everything about every person who hung around him for any extent of time. In a way, there was a small bit of belief left that if I dug deep enough, I could uncover information that could help me return the things and money I had given him over the extent of our crooked relationship. Once more my intuition spawned a sensation that guided my awareness towards a thought that the attempt will not be very successful. Despite what my senses told me, I decided to pursue the search.

Things were cooling down, the unnatural level of stress in me started to decline and I could grasp more free energy into what I considered reasonable. I sat in a comfortable position and closed my eyes. I went back to the very first evening I met him and started to observe the ongoing from a new perspective. Not to mislead, it didn't look or feel as if I was sitting next to myself, looking at everything as an innocent bystander. I was still seeing everything from my physical point of view in the same place where I was sitting or standing and the events were all the same as before. What was different though was my mindset. I already knew what was going to happen so now my focus was on things that back then slipped from my attention, therefore not giving me the full overview of the situation. I sat for a while reliving every moment I could recollect. Upon deeper observation his smirk started to make sense. He was feeling pleased whenever he saw me or someone fall for his lies. Suddenly every word he said sounded suspicious and eerie. I remembered the documents and screenshots he showed me. I started to question the validity of businesses he claimed to own, putting the non-disclosure agreement he made me sign under the biggest question mark. Mental notes were made.

Next we were in his car talking about his family and how his wife, kids and parents lived in the suburbs of my hometown. He was always picky with his words, obviously trying his best not to spill any revealing information. It was hard for him as due to callings of my intuition. I tried to study him as much as I could at any given moment and did my best to seem unsuspecting and harmless as I could. In a sense, it was simply exciting to observe an individual who was unlike anybody else I've met so far in my life. Somebody who was very unique yet not in an inspiring way, making him an engaging mystery. Slightly reminding a sociopath. As much as my intuition got to me, I was always testing him by asking certain questions. Playing along with him and not showing any emotions on my face while being kind or disappointed. Reading him was as puzzling as it was for him to understand my motives or ways of processing information. It's no secret that it was the result of my own decisions that led me down the path of being scammed and all, but even during my fall I managed to obtain valuable knowledge and experience.

The approach that I subconsciously employed gave me quite some insight into his world, giving me more clues on how to get to the bottom of his story.

I remembered all the names of people who I had encountered while I was out with him. One memory led to another and a recollection of locations in which I met them arose. The deeper I dug in my headspace, the more useful information I found, making my plan more realistic than before. We've had quite a long exchange of emails in which he had tagged me and other people who were supposed to attend his meeting. One of the first breaches that led me to discovering the whole story which was laying at the bottom of the piled up messages. Google is a beautiful, extensive and insecure platform which made it almost childishly simple to track down people who were tagged in his events.

It took minimal effort to get their contacts, locations and agreements to have a meeting, making the workflow almost perfect if not considering the reason why it was happening. I arranged meetings with all the involved people while Carmen was collecting information from his older victims. I composed a schedule with the people who were involved and followed through with it. During every step it got more to me that I wasn't going to find any valuable info from them and that besides getting to know people I was mostly throwing my energy into the void. Not only had nobody really known anything which could contribute to catching him. Most of them had already made peace with being used and tried to encourage me to do the same. By the end of my list, as I had finished my last meeting and was standing outside of a garage complex to which the man once brought me. Staring into the yellowish sky it became clear to me. The search for information was of no use. It was now my time to make peace with what I had gone through and I had to do it in depth. I was ready to accept it with every cell of my body.

DEPTH OF ACCEPTANCE

In my personal experience I've accepted things in different ways. Some things I accepted quickly and easily. Some other experiences took months or even years of deconstruction before I was able to make peace with them and carry on with my life.

As I stood there looking at the setting sun that was slowly falling behind tall living complexes and trees. I inhaled another mouthful of smoke, just enough to feel the difference but not enough to feel the scratch in the back of my throat. Upon exhaling I felt relieved. After all the hustle that took place during the last couple of months it was finally somewhat over. I was alive, I was in no danger and the damage that was caused was now only a reminder of caution. The weight I carried was no longer attached to me. I could finally feel how it fell off my shoulders. It felt as if my lungs were no longer squeezed together. I could finally take a deep breath. After a moment of letting it all sink in, my mind relaxed and became clear. I felt a new set of ideas arising in my head. Small impulses of thoughts wired through my awareness telling me that whatever had happened to me, had once again happened for my own good. Besides the minor physical and financial losses, it taught me many valuable lessons, showed me what people I should not work with and what types of people reside in the areas of my activity. I was no longer pissed and I was no longer eager to recover anything. The salty feeling that I held in me started to dissolve, making me neutral towards the idea of recovering the things that I lost. I was no longer interested in digging up info on him or going out of my way to find him. If he came around himself of course I wouldn't sit around doing nothing but that's not the same as constantly venting and wasting energy on visualising different scenarios that are only centered on that one person. I finished my doink and called the cab. I was done and I was now ready to go home and rest.

In the morning I felt refreshed and rested. My body was energised and my mind clear. Like the moment when you notice that your throat is no longer sore after a long illness, I appreciated the ordeal being over. I put all the thoughts linked to Arturs away, packed all the papers I collected and finally felt relieved. Most of the damage was already managed and my financial situation restored. The only thing that was lost permanently was my time and blind trust for random people. I spent enough time chasing him and I heard enough stories about his grand acts. It was time to source my energy and attention into other fields.

It was another reminder to me that if I desired to achieve something, I had to do it myself. Trying to get things done by sitting on other people's shoulders and using their money was not the route that was going to work out for me. Simply said, an easy way out was never an option for me no matter how many times I tried. The idea of starting a new business through assistance of investors was brushed away as it was now confirmed to be invalid with an approximate seven thousand euro loss. I decided to go back to the business I was good at. Though it was not yet registered as an official business, it was my primary source of income and it was a great one. From there I spent a while working on my orders. Everything was going as it was supposed to. I was making good money and had enough time to digest the lessons that I received during the past couple of months. The main lesson that I acquired, was to be clear with what I desire and to be able to provide for its growth through my own actions. I regained the peaceful feeling and was once again comfortable. The past experience was settling down and I was becoming more aware of how valuable it actually was. My awareness was slightly but notably sharper. I could recognise different patterns better and was much more confident in myself, as I now knew that I could handle much more than I could ever imagine.

I was minding my casual business when a notification sound went off in my phone. I wasn't engaged in any online conversations so I didn't expect any particular person to message me. I pulled the phone out of my pocket, making it light up its screen. After unlocking it and opening the messenger I pressed my finger against the unread window and to my surprise there was a message from the man who I thought I'd never see again. A feeling of amusement arose in my stomach followed by a grin. After finally letting go I didn't expect him to contact me. I wanted to reply to him. There were a million questions I wanted to ask and a thousand things I wanted to say. All of them exploded back into my awareness, turning into a mental storm that was eager to grow into a hurricane. To avoid making stupid decisions I stopped the stream of thoughts and recollected myself. Earlier I had spent a lot of energy imagining different scenarios of how I could capture him. To reduce the chances of blowing the freshly risen opportunity I had to play it right and not let emotions bet in between.

I had a quick evaluation of my options. Most of the things that I wanted to say were mostly emotion driven, aka if I pursued them I wouldn't achieve much. On the other side, bigger present of questions I had were also emotion driven and the answers wouldn't give me any closure or any valuable info. The only option that was left was to continue acting as if I had no clue about what was going on and hope that nobody told him that I was digging on him. I answered his question in the same confused manner as if I had no clue what was going on, adding that I was surprised by his extended absence. To my luck he had no idea of what I had known and not a single hint on what I had gathered on him. Just as expected he told me a semi believable story about how circumstances didn't work out for him and how different people backed out of their agreements, making it even harder for him to manage all the things he planned. I wasn't surprised, but continued playing along.

It was funny to talk to him knowing that everything he was saying was a lie. Then he added that if I no longer wanted to work with him he would understand it and wouldn't feel any type of way about it. To which I replied by being positive about continuing my work with him. After saying that I asked him about his whereabouts. Arturs was located in a neighbouring country and was about to return to the city where we met. I offered him to come over for another cup of tea so he could tell me in more detail about what had happened to him during the times that he was missing and to discuss, how our future work would look like.

According to his words he was going to be back by the next evening and if I was available he would come over. I told him that I was free that evening and was ready for him to be my guest. It was a great opportunity to finally catch him and get to actual results. Success was close, only a few steps away. I could almost feel the joy of seeing him sit uncomfortably answering the questions truthfully. There were a couple things left to do in order for the whole plan to succeed. Arturs was physically much bigger than me. To compare us roughly, it would take three mess, to compensate his weight. I needed someone to be there to back me up. Not to feel safe or to be aggressive with him but only so he wouldn't feel as comfortable as he would with me alone. I found a person who looked serious and intimidating enough and told them what was going on. The person agreed to help, so we arranged their arrival to be twenty minutes earlier than Arturs. Everything else was set up and the plan was ready to be pushed into action.

I was sitting on a couch and the person willing to help me sat on a chair. We were surrounded by a ringing silence, as there was nothing to talk about and I was more interested in hearing the doorbell ring rather than hearing anything else. It was still bright outside, the sun was on its way down shining its soft beams of light over the streets that were visible from the window. Occasionally I peeked out of it subconsciously hoping to see Arturs walk by but that never happened.

The only warning that I received was his message saying that he would arrive in five minutes. I told my guest and we change our positions. Now he was sitting on the couch and I was relocated to the chair waiting for the ring to hit my eardrums. As expected, it took him more than five minutes to arrive. Finally the doorbell started to ring and I rushed to the door. I pulled open the first door and then unlocked and pushed the second one. I didn't see him but heard his footsteps and heavy breathing. I decided not to stand in the doorway like an excited puppy, so I went back inside and stood in the corridor. It took him about a minute to get to the second floor and as he walked in, he forehead was sweaty and his breathing even heavier than before. In his hands he had a six pack that he placed on a counter before we shook hands. As he kneeled to untie his shoes, I started to ask him questions. In response I got a somewhat aggressive bark to not question him while he's getting undressed. *"Fair enough."* I thought to myself while shutting my mouth and walking to the kitchen. He followed me a minute later and on his way through the living room, he noticed the man sitting there. He greeted him without getting a response. That made him smirk in discomfort as he walked into the kitchen. He sat by the table and as I placed the teacups, I did the same.

Long and cringe worthy story short. He told me many unbelievable stories about his miraculous adventures and misfortunate events which led him to losing everything and coming back not on his luxurious car, but by bus. Then he told me about his grand plans of returning into the business but that got cut off by me and the man explaining to him that it was no longer convenient for me to support his lifestyle and that it was time for him to sign a paper with all the debts that he owed me. After a couple of attempts to clear his name with lies he understood that he was not going to exit the building before he signed it, and so he did.

It was somewhat pleasing to see him sweat and his eyes wander around the room as he was getting tangled in his own lies and through panic tried to come up with new lies. After all the time and stress I finally saw some sort of justice take place. The proper effort that the situation deserved was now given to it and the paper was signed. Knowing well, that he was not going to pay the whole amount right away and that it would take him a long time to pay everything even by pieces. I was simply satisfied by having his signature on the document, as it already provided enough proof and material to have him under control in case of a need. Another possible option was to make him work for me and do some dirty work in order to pay his debts but that idea got brushed away as it would have required too much unnecessary effort. After all, now I had everything I needed in case if I wanted to sue him. An hour long conversation/ interrogation was over. He was sweaty and nervous. All the beers that he brought stood untouched, but warm beer was probably the least of his problems. A short silence took place before I told him that it was time to leave. He quickly got up, grabbed his cans and rushed towards the door. In no time he had his shoes on and was exiting the door politely saying goodbye before shutting the door behind his back. I looked at the paper once more, took a photo of it and thanked the man for his assistance.

I was left alone in the apartment feeling somewhat great and relieved. It felt as if the universe sensed that I felt mistreated and out of generosity it gave me something to compensate what had happened. After that night I never heard of him again. As much as I know, he's a taxi driver somewhere in the city where everything went down. I no longer cared for him or for the losses. I felt satisfied with how the ordeal ended and was already into new ventures.

CHAPTER IV:
LITTLE COZY HOME

Things slowly nudged back into place and life got a bit easier for a moment. I set my focus on work and simultaneously our crew started to take our business more seriously. We made a list of things that could be improved in order to spend less time working and more time doing things we enjoyed. A good plan goes a long way and so it did. In no time our business was working like a clock and as that was happening, we could take in bigger orders and offer better products and services.

For example: During one meeting we were introduced to some nice eastern gentlemen who supplied us with great coffee beans for a friend's price. Making us great suppliers of quality coffee for many local roasters. Those as any other significantly good times didn't last too long but we weren't greedy. We managed to use that short period of time to make some profit and move into a mutual apartment. Living together was more convenient than living separately, so we went along with it and even formed our mutual bank or wallet. We had a nice two story apartment with a lot of space and cozy colourful lighting. Everyone had their own rooms, we had two bathrooms and a big living room with a projector. It didn't take long until the place felt like home bringing peace and relief every time we stepped through the door. It felt like a new beginning. As if everything was going to fall in perfect place any time soon and all the struggles we faced during the previous year were about to dissolve. It was around late August. Life was pure joy and excitement. The temporary home we had created was blooming. Flowering personalities communicating, learning and pursuing their goals and a happy pup running around the apartment, waving its tail and breaking all the soft toys it could get its paws on. My dear finally took up her dream of being a tattoo artist and started putting her energy into action. The boys and I got our shit together and started jogging in the morning and going to the gym a couple hours later. I was grateful and aware of what was going on.

I felt truly happy as I was living the dream that I had once pictured in my mind, though now it was much more complex and detailed. A glimpse of an understanding flashed in my awareness. *"This is why following Minds desires will never lead to true happiness. The mind and all its wants can't grasp the whole magnitude of any moment. It can't be aware of all the ongoing processes and details, so it can't picture or lead me to my true purposeful being."* As that crossed my mind, I became aware that this bypassing thought had a lot of value in it. I pondered it for a while pushing the logical mind towards some sort of a conclusion but came to nothing. It's hard to use logical thinking when trying to grasp something which has more properties to it than just linear movement in one particular direction. *"What could lead me to the true purposeful being?"* I asked myself. Then I snapped back into the present moment. I was seated behind a dining table with two of my companions sitting opposite to me. We discussed work while occasionally smoking and having some snacks. Something pointed our attention towards the calendar and especially the date. *18th of August* was close. The date of our first deal. The first relatively big financial loss I went through that essentially started this whole journey. I pointed it out and we laughed. The tone of our conversation changed to more melancholic. We looked back at all the experiences, events and situations that we went through. All the losses that we got ourselves into and later out of. All the profits that we managed to make and how not having a clear idea of how to grow that money passively spent on furniture and other things of not any significant importance. Another wave of appreciation washed over me, but this time I could see that others felt it too. One year matured all of us. We learnt to handle numerous issues that would have frightened us a year ago. It felt warm and encouraging as if the universe was telling us that if we endured those things in the past we were going to come out of anything that was yet to unfold.

Being in that blissful state was pleasant but the lack of challenges made it pretty boring quickly. Money and comfort were there but that was about all they were. Mere tools for transportation and getting things a bit easier. Achieving most of the goals that I had once set was also something I felt good about, yet that pleasure didn't last long either. With each day that passed, the itch in the back of my head got more on more present. Indicating that it was about time to set new goals.
To my surprise it wasn't as easy as I thought it would. Of course, it wouldn't be quite correct for me to expect something in the first place but still. I spent multiple days wondering and pondering what could be the next thing I would strive for. Nothing interesting came up. All the things I could think of were shallow and mostly material or dependent on something. That didn't work for me so I continued thinking. After a while of frustrating thoughts I decided to let it go. In the process of achieving my previous goals, growing and simply living life. I managed to lose my head to an extent and things once again started to look stressful and scary. I had an idea of direction where I was going with my life and the present moment I was in was pretty pleasant too so it wasn't critical for me to find new goals. Boredom did bother me but jumping head first into something I wasn't sure of was probably a worse idea than taking my time.

The only valid solution seemed to be the one where I relocate myself on my path. It wasn't something I was too excited about as it required a lot of energy and effort. Nevertheless there was no way over or around it. I decided not to rush into action so I let the idea of it sink in for a couple days. Mornings passed and so did the evenings after them. During which small situations and realisations started to point even more in the direction that I was about to travel.

RELOCATING THE SELF

Committing myself to this practice has helped me through many challenging times and has brought me clarity in times when nothing else was able to aid me. In case if this text starts to seem too spiritual. I would like to say that this practice is not something I would consider to go under the esoteric category. If I was to put a label on it, I'd call it mental deep cleaning. Simply speaking. If usually one doesn't have the time to look at their life from a distance and figure out what beliefs have outdated or what goals are no longer relevant to one. Reading and following through with this practice may help one do the described observation and if desired, bring in some changes. So in essence, it has the potential to help you clean up the mess you might have created and thus help you regain your energy and attention. Allowing you to channel that energy and attention in better and more fertile directions.

To start, it would be necessary to take a big sheet of paper. Smaller pieces papers and notebooks work too. Essentially anything you can write on and has enough space for you to relieve yourself on. On personal experience I've figured that usually there's more things that need handling than just one small sheet of paper. Though if so, the person who is in such a situation is quite lucky. Preferably take a pen full of ink, as you don't want to be bothered by ugly writing. That would take away your focus and make the process harder than it should be. Write down all the goals you've had for a while. The ones that you wish to achieve but think, that you aren't able to at the moment. The ones you've recently achieved.

The ones that you're pursuing at the moment. Ones that you really wish for but for some reason consider impossible.

At first you can start off by making a rough draft. It doesn't have to be clean and pretty right away. It's okay if at first it's a bit messy. Later you will rewrite your drafts into cleaner versions, as through that you will start and simplify the process of cleaning up the mess in your head.

Then write down everything you're grateful for. All of the things that you've once considered impossible and now have. Things you're simply happy to have in your life or to be around. Everything that brings you joy or makes you happy. You can go into detail and any depth you wish to. More things you are grateful for the better.

Then make a list of things that causes you discomfort, such as stress, worry and in general make you unhappy. Having them all written down in front of you will give you a clear overview of things that you don't wish to be attached to. All of that mess will no longer be in one big pile and you'll be able to start somewhere and continue your way down the list until everything is solved. Then hopefully you will no longer have anything bothering you and possibly with enough awareness to not get into any more big trouble.

By now you should have a more or less clear overview over majority of what make you happy keeps your focus away from your happiness and has the potential to make you happier and more wholesome. I'm not speaking of the results that will make you happy but mostly of the journey pursuing which makes you happy. Now you can start to think if you are happy with what you have achieved so far or if you're happy with your current position in life.

Personally, I often find myself being happy with what I have achieved and happy with where I am. Yet at the same time I have that clear feeling that there are many more things I wish to do or achieve that would make my living even more exciting.

If you're happy with what you've achieved and are happy with where you are. Appreciate that for a moment and you may continue setting your further goals or figuring how to get to your current goals in a more efficient way. If you're not happy with where you are right now. Deconstruct your position through the same questions and find substitutes or solutions to things that drain your happiness and then carry on to the next step. If you feel that you're not happy with anything. Then it might be useful to get to the bottom of why you're unhappy. What would be the reason for that, and how would your life be if you were happy. What would make you happy, and how to get away from things that don't make you happy? What would it take for you to become that happy person and then figure out the practical steps that will get you there. Truth be told, even awareness and understanding won't give you any results alone. Without you putting in the effort and using that knowledge in a practical form no progress will be done transmuting that knowledge into wisdom.

REORGANISING THE ORDER

I woke up early as usual, I had breakfast and a quick meditation session while going on about my morning routines. I felt refreshed and my mind was still clear. Reading some books in the past helped me to notice the thought-free frame between waking up and remembering my problems. After focusing on that, I learned to extend and enjoy it. While still being in that state it was the easiest to conduct any important actions. There were no thoughts that intervened, I took out a big sheet of paper and a pen filled with black gooey ink. The detail is not that important, I simply like to use black ink.

I wrote down my questions and things I desired to have and things I wanted to let go of. After a good couple of hours, the writings on the paper started to look like a solid map. Lines connecting the dots and new comments over dried ink. I started to scratch the surface. Some things started to clear up, revealing that there was much more work to do. I had created quite a mess in my head and for too long I didn't pay much attention to it. Well, there was no need for it and there are also many examples of people not dealing with their circumstances until it's too late. Because up to that late point the things didn't bother them enough for them to get to work. For a moment I felt frustrated, as if I opened a door to my home and found out that there was a huge party and everything was a mess. Not a nice sight to see, but it was my home and there was nobody else to clean it up but me. I continued writing and pondering. It took a lot of time and energy. Each time that I started to get tired, things got confusing again. That's how I knew, that I was out of energy and it was time for me to take a break. In the past I've done similar things but back then they didn't take that much time. Once again I had expected that it would take me a day tops. Though the amount of mess wasn't as small as I expected the process ended up taking more than a week. Of course I wasn't able to spend the whole week solely digging up my mind.

I had to do other things too and as a result, managed to spend only a couple hours a day deconstructing. Each day was came with result though, binging some clarity and understanding back to me. After a month still I hadn't finished the process. It turned out to be a much bigger venture, than just cleaning up my head. I had grown and matured. It was time for me to pick a grander path and I had to do it wisely. The practice that I thought was going to give me simple clarity was slowly opening my eyes to a whole new world that due to my old hustles and struggles was hidden away from my attention.

With each day that I attended my practice I managed to cut off some old beliefs and grudges. I got to let go of some misunderstandings and relive some events that kept bothering me long after they ended. It felt great. I got to see, that there was much more available to me and that if I could only throw away all the old things, I would be able to completely open myself up to new opportunities and possibilities.

It was exhausting and yet pleasant. Like working out in the gym but internally. I could feel how my mind became more flexible and less stressful. Things started to make sense again and I no longer felt anything about things that once annoyed me or made me uncomfortable for no apparent reason. I started to become more aware of myself and how things I considered unimportant were actually unhealthy. Action always leads to a reaction, so as intended I had more energy that I was able to channel into bettering myself and my perspective at life. Maybe I've mentioned previously how whenever I decide to improve something in me or decide to channel my attention to some internal issues. All those things suddenly start to come to surface. My passive aggressiveness egoistic issues need for control. all that started to pop up in my face like acne. I knew that this was going to happen but once again I didn't think that it was going to be that severe. Nevertheless, it was a path I had to walk so I continued.

My issues started to pop up everywhere. In my personal life as well as work, making it inevitable for me to deal with them. Everything was in my head in the first place, so there was nowhere I could possibly escape from it. Not struggling against it was something I learned through my past experiences, when I struggled and fought against changes and managed to get myself into even bigger trouble. After being hit on my head multiple times. I came to a conclusion, that it was easier to face my problems and internal issues, then run from them. They would never struggle catching me anyway, as they were always right there with me ready to eat me or be dissolved.

Changing my attitude became one of the most valuable skills I developed throughout this journey. By changing my attitude, I mean getting to the very bottom of my beliefs, habits and patterns. Learning to understand how they function, how they react to things and how they affect me and my surrounding. Of course it wasn't easy at first but with time and very sensible necessity, I learned to enjoy it and got more artistic with it. From my previous experiences, I knew that the process was good for me. So going through it turned into an interesting challenge, rather than a curse that I had to endure. The results were significant as well, so I always felt compelled towards pursuing that path and staying on the course. With each step that I took I could see improvements in my mentality and my physical body. I felt more energised and alive. As the progress continued, the mind started to ask questions. *"How soon is the finish line?" "How far are we?" "When are we getting rewarded?"* The mind always wants explanations. It doesn't accept *"Don't know"* for an answer. It would rather make up a false truth than accept that something is unknown to it. Being aware of that doesn't guarantee any results on its own but does offer an ability to change something. Figuring that the path that I had taken was as long as my life and maybe even longer *(meaning that my decisions will affect my children and possibly grandchildren)*, I found a way to accept that I would never know the true percentage of my progress. That I was always going to find things I could gain, fix or improve.

If we're speaking spiritually, the path became a natural part of me. Not something separate but something I was. Something I walked every day when I was awake or asleep. Casually speaking I got used to and found joy in working on myself. The process became my daily activity. Thus making progress my main goal and allowing me to stay on a more or less constant way up. Of course downfalls were and are a natural part of the process but they are not something significant to write about.

OLD FRIENDS NEW CIRCUMSTANCES

When everything goes well, we often stop being attentive and completely surrender ourselves to joy. Essentially that's what we are here for but due to our egoistic nature we often get carried away in the wrong direction. Enjoying things that end up abusing us. The same goes for me. Our situation was on a constant rise. The new lifestyle I was living was improving my physical body and my mental state. We had bettered our work system so now we had to spend even less time working while making twice as much money. At that time nothing was really bothering me. Sometimes I had some thoughts about pursuing new goals or making my current ones more interesting, but besides that nothing. I let my guard down and my attention focused on other things. My moral compass and gut were of course still wide awake but without attention those weren't as useful as usually.

One quiet evening, when we were all home. Some of us were in the kitchen cooking, others cleaning up the table and preparing the tableware. The atmosphere was peaceful and relaxed. All of us acknowledged it and embraced it to the fullest. Peace and relaxation weren't the kind of things we could feel very often because of the nature of our work, but we didn't complain much. For the same reason I often got carried away with thoughts about work and wasn't always able to shift my attention from stressful topics to soothing peace at home. Being surrounded by my closest friends, people who I consider my second family. I could really let go of all the worry that surrounded our work on a daily basis and truly enjoyed the beautiful carnival of jokes and smiles that was going on in our living room. When all the dishes were prepared, served and eaten. We continued sitting behind the table, chatting and joking about all the things that happened to us in the past couple weeks and what we expected to happen in the near future. After a while, our conversation took a direction in which we were discussing our possibilities to grow the money we were currently holding. A mutual agreement was reached that it wasn't good to simply hold money and do nothing with it. It was only right to make the money work for us, but we had to do it in the right way. First we thought about investing into some businesses that were owned by people around us.

The idea itself was ambitious but when we looked at the people who were around us we didn't see many in who we really wanted to invest our hard earned cash in. Other options that we had was to invest in our friend who owed us money. That way he could make some money quicker, being able to repay back the investment as well as his debt. He's been our friend for past two years and together we've gone through quite some adventures. On some occasions he helped us out and on others we gave him a hand. There were times when we owed him money because of our own problems. This time he owed us. The opportunity that we were looking at was simple and yet promising enough to follow it. We though it through and to an extent, believed that there weren't many things that could go wrong. After all, he was our friend. We trusted him and knowing that he was going through a rough path we wanted to help him out. We weighted our options and figured that in two days, we should have the investment and the debt paid back to us. After exchanging looks we decided to contact our friend and offer him our idea.

The upcoming day we met him in the heart of our hometown. After quick handshakes and lighter sparks, we got straight to the business. Our offer resonated with him quickly. He said that he appreciated our approach and that with our help he was indeed able to get his things straight and pay us back. We asked him how soon could he start and the reply was expected. He was ready the next day. Nothing was telling us that it wasn't a good idea. A couple other opportunities popped up at the same day but they were more or less equal to the one we were going with. We decided not to shift plans and carried on.

We sent him a message the next afternoon. In a couple hours probably as he woke up he sent us a reply. A meeting was arranged as usually and soon we were standing face to face with each other. We gave him the envelope with our investment and he packed it in the left internal pocket of his coat. The details were already known to everyone, so just to be clear we quickly went over them one last time. Our friend, who looked like a soviet school teacher, mixed with a Russian thug and a samurai tied his hair in a knot, fixed his glasses and started going. We looked at each other and almost synchronically said *"Hope it goes well."* After a small pause we got dressed and left the location. That day we didn't speak to our friend anymore as seemingly there was no need for that. We did get a couple messages from people who were presenting other opportunities but after explaining to them what was going on they didn't get back to us. It seemed slightly weird, but we didn't make a big deal out of it.
Not suspecting a thing we went on about our business without any second thoughts.

Maybe our first mistake was investing seventy perfect of our whole bank into our friend, hoping it would pay off. Back then we didn't think about it. The fact that we gave most of our money away meant that we weren't able to invest in other areas and weren't able to get as many things for ourselves as we may have wanted. Then we weren't bothered by it and simply decided to dismiss those thoughts. When the time we agreed upon passed, we decided to shoot our friend a message asking him if everything was alright. We waited for a couple hours, suspecting that he was still asleep as it was still pretty early. More hours had passed and still there were no new messages in our inbox. Okay we thought maybe it's a similar situation to the one that happened with him during our last venture. When he went missing for five days and turned up on the other end of the country near the Russian border with a new phone and an amazing escape story.

THE STORY OF ROMAN

Before I go on with the main narration, I believe this story is worth sharing. The fact that it happened a long time ago makes it safe enough to share. Plus this story may be nothing more than a figment of his or my imagination. Possibly making it nothing more than simple fiction.

The last time we interacted with Roman we gave him some money with a request to grow it for us. He gets a percent of the profit for himself and pays his debt. Without our knowledge he decided to go to his mob related friends and got himself into an exciting adventure. By giving our money to Roman we turned our cash into two keys and had them flipped. Alright. It's a common procedure that happens behind the curtains. It's not something we would get upset about. Then again we had no clue that the process would involve a whole palette of unexpected events. As it turns out, while he was growing our investments. He managed to sit in the back of a car with those two keys while the driver was a mob with no driver's license. Of course a police patrol happened to stop them and asked them for their papers. As it was mentioned above, the gentleman didn't have any papers in his possession but did have two keys in the trunk. Probably one thought led to another and the man decided to press the gas. For a while, they were chased in the suburbs close to the border of the city. After some time they managed to get away from the police for what it turned out to be about five minutes. Maybe even less considering the rush of adrenaline, that was probably rushing through their systems. Our friend got both of the keys shoved in his backpack and got dropped off the next moment. The driver sped off and was caught about twenty minutes later.

Considering the local laws and the fact that you can bribe local law enforcements. Plus taking into consideration that the man behind the wheel had no license which could be taken. He got off with a small fine and had to take a cab back home.

Later we found out that the event wasn't even a big deal for the man. For him it was a common practice to change cars every two weeks. What sounded like a total action movie to us, turned out for him a minor inconvenience. Our friend hid for a while and made his way to the closest person he had in the city. The most trusted friend that could come to his mind. He went to his door and rang the bell. To Romans luck his friend was home and welcomed him right in. Roman explained his situation and they agreed that the friend would take him to another city. In the dark of the night they started to move. Upon his arrival, he laid low at his parent's house for the next couple of days. When he felt more or less calm he took another trip to a bigger city nearby that was right by Russian border and bought himself a new phone.

It was now about one o'clock in the morning. We were all tired and worrying about our friend Roman was no longer that urgent. It was late and there was no point in letting those thoughts eat on us. Nothing would have changed if we continued stressing that night so we decided to go to sleep and see what tomorrow would bring. By the time we all got to our bedrooms and started to wander off into the peaceful realm of sleep, the thoughts about Roman faded away. Suddenly David's Voice breaks out into a scream alerting all of us. It was loud but due to layers of closed doors it was muffled. It was a quick *"Roman is alive!"* that made us all jump up and spawn in David's room. A wave of excitement washed over me, completely sobering my mind. Our first question was *"Roman, did you die?"* to which he replied with a casual *"Almost."*

After some messaging we found out that he was going to be back the next evening but only if we could arrange him a driver and a car. A simple request meaning that we had to find someone who was willing to travel all the way to him, pick him up with whatever he possibly had with him and safely bring him all the way back. Considering the trouble he might have gotten into, maybe not the safest trip to undertake. Again the luck was on our side and we managed to find the right person just in time. The road trip went well, without any further complications and we got the money we wanted to grow.

OLD FRIENDS NEW CIRCUMSTANCES II

Coming back to the main plot, the previous story should shed some light on why we trusted Roman with our money and why we didn't get all worked up right away. We didn't get any responses from him. Not a single message or a sign that he has even been online. For the sake of comedy we decided to make bets on how soon he was going to come up again and what could be the reason for this disappearance. During the next few days we slowly started to get worked up and worried. It wasn't only that our friend was missing with a significant amount of our money. Besides that, it was also about us wanting to grow further but being held back by a lack of finances that was of course our own fault. On top of all that, things with our business started to go down as the season was coming to an end. We needed to make money to secure our wellbeing for the approaching winter. It was about time to do something.

Like always we showed our emotions further away from the present moment. In cold blood we started to handle whatever needed to be taken care of. It was our casual routine to get things fixed no matter what and only complain to ourselves about it. Despite the experiences from my past life I noticed how we always managed to get things solved no matter what. Through our regular work methods we slowly started to make our money back while being more responsible with it. The effort that it took to make back what we had given was already exhausting enough. We didn't have much energy nor time to look for our friend. So we hung that situation in the closet. While work took up most of our time we still managed to meet many people daily. Some of our mutual friends told us that Roman left with our money and wasn't planning on coming back nor returning it. At first I took those comments for jokes. Once again, I didn't want to believe that a friend of mine could do something like that. After all we went through a lot together. To me it didn't make sense.

In addition to that, later I discovered a fragment of a reason why I didn't want to accept that scenario. It was always floating on the surface but previously I didn't pay attention to it as seemingly there was no need for it. The fact that he had the same name as my father had created some unnecessary trust for him. On its own, it pulled my guard down and later became an obstacle. The problem with it was that it didn't let me look at the situation clearly but put a filter of affection over my perception.

Next couple of days were busy with meetings. Some of the people we met happened to be our mutual friends. While conversing with them, we sometimes asked questions about Roman, trying to figure out what happened to him and things of such kind. Most told us that they had no clue but some slipped and revealed some new information. Some people told us that he went on a vacation but couldn't specify the country. Besides, multiple individuals told us that he departed but all of them gave out different countries. When we found that out we finally accepted that once again we were left with nothing. At that point it was already funny. It was bittersweet but acceptable. After all there was no other option but to accept whatever happened. We had gathered enough info to start pondering our next moves. When we looked at whatever we had collected logic got its moment of recognition. It was clear, that the amount of money he had taken wasn't enough to start a new life. He also lacked a solid plan that allowed him to escape easily. It was certain that after a while he was going to come back. The questions were when was he coming back and what was going to happen next? We couldn't know for fact, when he was going to return so that was a big unknown X. Only thing left, was to try and come up with a plan that would hopefully return us the lost money.

We were hoping to find a solution and get back what we had given, but whenever we were honest with ourselves. We knew that by the time he comes back all the money will be drained. Indeed it was an unpleasant realisation. Especially considering that we gave him a couple of thousands. Nevertheless he was a grown man, or at least was making a grown man's decisions. Coming from that he should be able to make that money back and return it like the grown man he was. I remember myself sitting back and quietly evaluating that even though the amount of money was pretty serious. I wasn't a violent person, nor a person who would value money over people's wellbeing. I didn't want a person who I had considered my friend to get hurt. Indeed it was an unpleasant situation and he had to face the consequences. But in my mind, as he didn't harm us in a serious way I didn't want him to get seriously hurt either. I wanted to believe, that no matter what he or we would find a solution in how he could make everything back without any injuries. The other guys didn't approve of my thoughts as much. When I was explaining my point of view they said that he knew what he was doing and as he wasn't unfamiliar to that business. He also knew what he was getting himself into. They did accept that if he would give back everything he owed us, nothing would happen to him. That gave me a small sense of peace, but that too got quickly shut down. Ian opened his mouth as soon as I stopped talking to take a break and told me that it was highly unlikely that Roman would have the money by the time he would be back. Making the plan wasn't of utmost importance as we knew we still had time. Personally I was okay with letting go of that money. I made peace with it a while ago. But David and Ian weren't on the same page with me. For them it was a cold business and a matter of not letting people walk over us whenever they wanted to.

BACKWASHED

When things start to go down, they do so with great magnitude. One thing after another our situation started to spiral out of control. As I described previously we had lost a couple thousands. The next slap from the Universe came in a form of a call. One beautiful evening Ian's mother got a call. She was asked about her son. When she asked the caller about what was going on she got told that he was in serious trouble. As I found out the same evening as I was writing this book behind our kitchen table. It turned out that the local police had reopened an old investigation on him and to top that off, opened up two new cases in addition.

An unexpected and crushing blow that shook all of us. Not only my lack of knowledge about him being involved with such things potentially endangered our whole family, we were also low on money and it was not our season. We barely had the money to get by after paying all of our bills and subscriptions. Now we were also face to face with the biggest problem we have seen so far. It wasn't just new and frightening but also looked like it was about to be very expensive. I put away all my notebooks and pens. The moment was no longer suitable for writing. It was now time to have a serious conversation. We had to figure out what those news meant in every way possible. What it meant for Ian and what it meant for our family and business. We were in a need for a new solid plan. It had to be clear and free from any breaches. This time we were in a situation where mistakes were unacceptable.

That meant if anything went wrong, any small thing nudged from the plan, then our dear brother would end up in jail.

Observing from the side the situation might seem pretty dark. Obviously there's not much fun in being investigated by police or possibly being put to jail. A rather grim picture overall. Nevertheless it turned out to be one of the most fun times full of sarcastic jokes, mockery and heartfelt confessions. During those couple of days, I got to observe Ian very closely and got to know him much better than ever before. The first thing that erupted my mind was when he told me that those final news were what he was secretly hoping for. For him it meant that there was nothing left to hold him down in this country. He felt as if he could finally go and travel, see what the world had to offer outside of the borders of our small country. What would be a frightening news for some turned out to be a gesture of encouragement for him. He accepted it happily and was ready for whatever was about to happen. For those few days that he had left to live here, he wanted to get the most out of them. To feel everything as if it was happening for the first time. Capturing it in his memory as clearly and firmly as possible.

Though Ian was considered to be the most organised it only looked like it on the surface or when it came to those few tasks he was truly gifted at. When it came to daily routines and things that were based on basic social experiences were completely alien to him.
For example: He learned to tie his laces when he was seventeen. He was twenty when he had to leave and even then he barely had any idea about how to wash his clothes or how to use kitchenware properly.
For the sake of his own good and mostly survival. Me and David decided to get him ready ourselves. That meant us planning out his escape route and all the transportation stops and papers he would or wouldn't take with him. As he was an escaping fugitive it wasn't very good for him to carry his ID's with him. It also meant that we would pack his backpack,

including the necessary clothing, survival gear, money, electronics and things which would be his essentials in a completely unfamiliar place. Ian wasn't very prepared for a situation of such kind. He didn't have a proper backpack, any camping gear or any survival knowledge nor anything that would aid him in a foreign country. All of those things had to be bought and taught to our dear little brother, meaning that we needed money. Of course at that time money wasn't something we were in an abundance of. Like always we had to find a way. We decided to hit up all the people who owed us anything and try to get their debts back as soon as possible. Another path we pursued simultaneously, was selling as many useless things as possible. Of course we announced a big discount season through our company which also contributed with some quick income. Lady Luck smiled to us and we managed to get some debts collected and some orders filled. That boosted us to a couple of thousands, instantly granting us a bit more hope. It already seems to be an unspoken rule, that every time something significantly good happens to us and we lose our guard for a moment, we'd get slapped right in the face.

Even though I could see, how our brother was present in every moment he was in. From his very awakening up until he closed the door of his room, I could feel how he was enjoying every second with his girlfriend. Every bite that he took could be seen reflecting in his face. It was mesmerising to watch someone be in that state, despite all the chaos that was going on around him.

LAUGHING IN THE FACE OF DANGER

Three days before Ian's departure around lunch. I was once again sitting behind the kitchen table minding my business, when David and Ian came through the door rushing towards me. Their eyes were wide and I could see them being very excited. The excitement was different from the usual though. It was more of a worried excitement or extreme alertness. They quickly pulled chairs from behind the table on the opposite side of me and sat down. By that time all of my things were already put away as if by habit I already knew. I couldn't be doing two things at the same time. I noticed how both of their hands were shaking. Before they started to engage in a conversation with me, *"What's the bad news?"* I asked. They looked at each other and started laughing. I felt a tingle in my stomach. No matter how bad the news could be, they could still make me laugh. David once mentioned that we have developed an interesting skill. We're able to see something good in every situation no matter how bad it gets and in addition to that. We've also learned to profit out of every seeming loss.

"We bribed the local DEA." They said synchronically. I was baffled. I wasn't ready to hear that. I sat back for a second in silence and burst out laughing. *"Was that the bad news?"* I asked again? *"The bad news is that we have to pay a couple more thousands now. And we have to pay them by tomorrow morning."* Said David. It meant that now we were once again out of money and were barely able to sustain ourselves while sending him away. The same evening we got hit with another news from the same source. It turned out that possibly somebody found out that the info was given to us and that now the police wanted to question Ian as soon as possible. That

made us slightly more concerned. We had even less time and barely any money at all. As if by a bizarre miracle, we had all the money we needed by the morning and everything went well. Money got paid off and Ian returned safely.

Two days before departure, Ian decided to go see all his close family members and say goodbye to them. He left home around noon and came back only in the very late evening. During that day I received all of his valuable contacts and some information on what to do regarding his situation and what should be told to people in case if any questions were asked. That day I didn't do much. Most of the things on my behalf were done and I wanted to rest for a moment. I felt a need to recollect myself and get my mind straight again. All the commotion and events messed me up a little, exhausting and stressing me out. I rested and spent some time by myself, organised mi inner world and took a walk around the woods.

That day I remembered how I once thought about what would it be like to be in Ian's shoes. What would it be like to see the world from his perspective? What would it be like to make decisions considering the options and possibilities he possessed? When that thought returned to my mind it made me laugh once more. I understood that the exact thing I once thought about was about to become reality to its utmost extent. Then I came to realise that it wasn't only about having his possibilities, opportunities and contacts but that I was also about to take care of his responsibilities and everything that came along with him. I was cool with it and felt ready. I knew that I was able to take care of all those things and people, that were about to be put on my shoulders. It didn't bother me.

I was excited for the new experiences and felt as if I could make something good out of everything that was going to be in my reach. On the other side, I remember clearly how sadness got to me from time to time. In those few months that we lived together. We formed a lovely family. I appreciated our little household very much, as it was something I've always wanted to be a part of. In the light of recent events, a lot of that joy got lost in worry and none of us were truly able to embrace that lovely atmosphere.

In a way it was hollowing to see how after being thrown around by waves one was being torn away from us. It wasn't only about Ian's departure, but his girlfriend, who was brought from another city and now wasn't able to come along with him right away. I felt sympathy for her, all of us did. We all acknowledged the fact that she was staying with us and that she was about to have a hard time. She had the hardest time accepting the situation in the first place and took it pretty personally. Knowing her emotional problems at the time we knew that she would need a lot of support and over watch. Though all of us knew those issues were present we didn't discuss them much. Probably because we had other things in mind and seemingly more important things to take care of. The thought of it didn't give me nor my girlfriend a lot of peace. She was already a part of our small family and leaving one of us in a bad state was no option. I made a mental note that if I noticed her struggling with something or simply being antisocial for some reason, I would try to reach out to her.
I thought about it a bit more and decided to go with that plan. If I was already taking over the leadership in our business might as well lead at home. At least if I'm watching over everything myself I don't have to worry about things being not done.

One day before Ian's departure we were occupied with many activities. Matter of fact, we had so many things to do we had to arrange different tasks to each one of us. Even though we had evenly split all the tasks, it took almost the whole day for all of us to get those things done. An interesting practical thing we brought out from that day, was when we were packing our immigrants clothes. Jokingly we tried vacuum sealing his clothes. Sucking out all of the air from the package seemed like a funny enough thing to do, but as a result we discovered a very compact way to pack underwear. We ended up taking only about forty percent of the original space required and the little bricks of underwear we ended up with, were quite amusing too. While I and David were preparing Ian's belongings, he himself went to meet all of the people he had to say goodbye to. We didn't see him the whole day. He probably wanted to see as many people as possible, to hold away unnecessary confusion. Considering that people have different schedules and it was in the middle of a week, he probably had to wait for some time before people turned up. That day, he returned late, just before midnight hit. The following hours were interesting to experience, yet hard to describe. In the moment, I could feel bliss and happiness from seeing how all of us were enjoying the time together. Cheerful voices, music, scents of different dishes and rapid clicking of our dogs nails on the floor. Everything was happenings as if in slow motion. At the very same time I could clearly feel heaviness echoing through my being. There was also a note of sadness which sometimes rang through the room. It was very subtle and quiet and yet it was there. Representing the division that was approaching us. We went to sleep in peace that night. It didn't take me long to fall asleep. I didn't have much on my mind and the late hours urged me to pass into dreams.

On the day of Ian's departure things didn't go as planned at all. We woke up early, ready to finish the last steps and seat him in the car. After a nice breakfast we were hit with the next big news. The police wanted to see him as soon as possible as in regards of something of utmost importance and hurry. Once again throwing wood in our already big bonfire we thought we had no time to waste. We jumped up and got ourselves dressed. I started to manage my communication with the driver, to get him going earlier and made sure all of his things were packed. There was no time to go back if anything stays behind, so I wanted to be extra sure that nothing was missing. While I was handing those things the guys went to finish their last tasks in the city. The driver was ready in a couple of hours and the dudes were back home soon after leaving. Everything was packed and our traveler was ready for his new adventure into the unknown.

Our whole family gathered around and we hung out for some time and chatted about how we were planning to start communicating with him as soon as he arrived.

How we would visit him during the New Year's Eve and possibly move there soon after. It was pleasant and reassuring. I tend to think that those conversations made him feel more certain and confident. Knowing that even in such times he had people who were always there for him. The car was arriving in twenty minutes. There was no time left. After Ian set his foot out the door he wasn't ever going to return to that place. We walked to a nearby hotel where the driver had to pick them up. There were a couple more minutes left, because the car was a little late, so we spent those last moments smoking and talking. During that brief conversation, I told him that he didn't need to worry and that I would take care of his girlfriend as long as I had to and when the time was right, I was going to send her on her way to him. He was about to ask me for the same thing so as I said the words for him he simply smiled. After recollecting his thoughts he said that it was now time for me to take over all of the responsibility and that he knew that I would manage. We thanked each other as the car pulled up by our side. In the window we saw a familiar face that smiled at us and we smiled back. After exchanging hugs, Ian and David entered the car and drove off. Me and Ian's girlfriend looked at each other and went back home.

As we walked back in the apartment felt much emptier though it was the same. It was quiet and no longer had the same energy as before. It was the same space it was half an hour ago. The same place we called our home and yet so different. Part of that spark that kept our home warm was now missing.

I made peace with his absence around second or third day. Of course I could feel the difference and many things reminded me of him as we did a ton of things together. Besides being aware of him not being around, it didn't bother me.

I had enough on my plate and I was confident in what I was doing so I didn't have a need nor time to seriously feel some type of way about his absence. The same couldn't be said about his girlfriend though. For Kate, the first two weeks were the hardest. For her it was difficult to accept his absence.

She blamed herself and was mad at him and the whole world for what had happened. She found no joy in things or even simply being as at that time her life was revolving around loving him. As the object of her love was gone, so was her happiness. She barely ate and didn't engage in conversations on her own. There were days when she didn't even leave her room. She hated her job and the fact that she had moved because of her boyfriend which was no longer there for her. There wasn't even a chance to communicate with him until he made it to his destination and she had no clue how long it would take him to get there. She felt tired and alone.

ROUGH SEPARATION

As I had promised, I was there to support her. Or at least I tried to give my best while not being annoying or too friendly. From personal experience I learnt that it's not helpful at all when people are trying to be too helpful or supportive. I tried talking to her whenever she came out and offered her to hang out with us. To cook all together, to watch a movie or any other communal activity we could all engage in. After a while she became more talkative and started sharing her thoughts and feelings. She opened up about what was bothering her and how she was feeling because of it. I told her about my experience with attaching my happiness to external sources and that I've felt in a similar way when I was confused or didn't have something to do with myself. That seemed to help a bit as I saw that she started to think in a slightly different pattern. Of course such changes never happen instantly and can never be forced from the outside, so I gave her as much time as she needed. I also said that if she had any questions or needed any guidance she could always ask. If I was able to give her any valuable advice I would happily do so.

The next couple weeks I could observe major improvements in her being. She was smiling more and was no longer pale. The job that she hated had drained her enough so she finally collected her courage and went to her bosses to quit. Leaving the job made her much happier than I thought. When she came home telling us that she was no longer working for that company she was jumping and dancing across the living room.

Finally after about a month of Ian being away, he finally got into steady contact with us. He could now communicate with us almost nightly, as that was the time when he was at a gas station with Wi-Fi or one of his roommates was around to share a hotspot. Being able to talk to him again made Kate very happy. She could hear his voice and he could hear hers. They exchanged hour's long voice recordings nightly. I could still hear her record or listen to them when I woke up.
It warmed my heart every time she shared those moments with me through little flaunts like *"Guess who got a message from a fugitive?"* The atmosphere in our home calmed down. Slowly starting to go uphill again. When Kates period of hardship started to pass and a danger of her committing suicide was no longer present. I finally felt as if I got a breath of fresh air. For once our home was at peace and everything was more or less fine.

Did I say that everything was more or less fine? Yeah… That's what I thought. A couple days later, I wake up to a message from a mutual acquaintance. After a rollercoaster that was my life for past one and a half years. I learnt to love and suspect the blinking blue light on my second phone. The blinking light had only one main function which was to notify me if the owner of the messages landed in the inbox. For me though, it meant one of two things. Either I was about to get paid or something was wrong. By wrong I mean things not going by the plan or causing distress to any parties involved in the process.
Repeated experience taught me how to be neutral towards the blinking light. The reason why I'm bringing this up right now is because if we look at it from a habitual point of view. If the blue light had always indicated bad news. Seeing it would instantly trigger negative emotions and processes, as the mind has already learnt a pattern. If the blue light always indicated good news, it would repeat a similar process following a positive pattern. Learning to be neutral towards it and not letting habits or emotions come in between came in very handy. It simply saved me from wasting a lot of energy. I picked up the phone

and tapped the screen sixty-three times, entering the password and unlocking it. After entering the second password, I could see the message and its author. The message was set to be destroyed in five minutes. I had already opened the window with the message. He now knew that I had seen his message and I had no other option but to read it.

IAN'S PRESENTS:
"A little frustrating but manageable."

It started with something about Ian and his whereabouts. Following the question came a statement, saying that our fugitive owed him around three and a half thousands and that the person was eager to get his money back as our friend wasted enough time not paying him. Great news to receive early in the morning. Not only that I had no idea about Ian holding such a debt. It now seemed to me that it was now put on my shoulders. *"A little frustrating, but manageable."* I thought to myself smirking. Well I chose the path so I was in no position to complain. There was no point in complaining either. A mere waste of energy and thought. Maybe through some struggle but a solution would be found and everything would be resolved just like always. I then took away my attention from the news and decided to mind my business until everyone else woke up.

When the rest of our remaining gang woke up and crawled out of their rooms. We gathered in the kitchen for breakfast. By the time everybody got to the first floor and inhabited the kitchen. I decided it was time to start talking. I had no desire to engage in a conversation of that kind so early in the morning. Possibly ruining the moment for others to some extent. What was news to me was no news to others though. They knew Ian had debts and the one I found out about wasn't the only one. There was one more debt of the same size that he was holding. Others expressed their displeasure with the situation but also accepted it and agreed to help. Gladly the discussion didn't faze anybody and we carried on with our morning routine.

The next couple of days were pretty casual. Me and David were filling in orders to make some money and keep our customers and partners interested.

The fact that we had no actual business registered yet meant that we had no contracts and thus had to constantly stay on top of our game to maintain relevancy. My girlfriends tattoo business finally started to take off just the way she hoped and so everyone was occupied. I was sitting in a cafe writing rough drafts for this book, when suddenly my phone rang. Not many people have my contacts and ones that do don't call me without a need. So an unexpected call surprised me. When I pulled it out and looked at the screen, it said Ian's Dad. *"For what reason could he be calling me?"* I thought to myself. Either something happened or Ian's mother was stressing him out for some reason. I slid my thumb across the screen and put the phone to my ear. One could expect that both of those options were happening at the same time. First thing we discussed was Ian's mothers concern with him. Though he did go to see her before leaving. Somehow he managed to leave her an impression that he was about to kill himself. She couldn't reach him and the friends of his that she asked had no clue themselves. Many odd thoughts can invade the mind of a mother when she lets worry and uncertainty get to her. He told me that he didn't know what to tell her because he was afraid to tell her the truth. I told him that if it was too difficult for him I could do it myself. At first he didn't want me to do it finding reasons why it shouldn't happen, but before even letting me agree to not intervene. He told me that he actually did want me to do it. I laughed and agreed. Getting to the second topic wasn't as fun as the first one. I heard, that he got a call from Ian's probation officer and the officer's supervisor or something. He was told, that if Ian didn't turn up by the end of the month, he was going to be listed as internationally wanted.

When the father asked the officer, how serious was his son's status. The reply was pretty logical yet equally concerning. It stated that Ian was going to be wanted all across Europe. Not a worldwide status, but still a relatively big area where to be wanted. There wasn't much we could discuss through the phone. There was a big possibility that both of our phones were tapped.
Even if they weren't all the calls going through operators were recorded and could be accessed at any time anyway. I played it off like I was surprised and had no clue about the news.
The acting had to be clean in real life and on the record. I told him that if his son was indeed going to turn up behind my door, I was going to inform him. Before finishing the call we agreed to meet some time later.

It was a pretty important matter. I thought about it for a while and decided that it would be the best to meet Ian's dad the same day. After a little more pondering I came up with an excuse to call and meet him to make it as natural as possible. I rang his phone and we agreed to meet at his home later in the evening. The same day a couple more things came up so I was actively occupied until the very time I had to see him.
It was already dark when my cab arrived to the tall Soviet building. The long towering building which looked like a circuit on a motherboard reminded me of my old home where I once lived with my parents and my grandmother. Warm memories once again flooded my heart, offering me a trip back to the past. I would have enjoyed that small treat from my mind but there was no time for that. The mind reminded me why I had come to that house and that my time was limited. I rang the bell and after a couple second the outer door opened. I tried to calculate to which floor I have to take on the elevator. After not being able to figure it out by the time I got into the elevator, I decided to take a guess. I got to the right floor and for a minute I stood behind the door. A sound of a key entering a lock vibrated in front of me. Then came a twist and two turns, a knob yanked downwards and the door opened. In front of me

stood a much older version of Ian. We greeted each other outside of his apartment. He looked jumpy and in his voice, I could clearly hear worry. He didn't know what to say to his wife. Even though he knew about his son's criminal past. The mother had no clue. For all that time she thought that her son was making money from bitcoins and reselling coffee beans to roasting facilities. He looked at me and asked if I had a plan of any kind. I didn't but was confident I could make something believable up on the spot. In my pocket I also had a backup plan. It was a small 8GB memory stick with one audio file on it. It was a recording which Ian made for his mother a couple days prior. In it he explained to his mother what was going on and why he left. As he told me he was completely clear and honest in it. Though his dad didn't approve of my improvisation idea at first, after I explained the backup plan his mind changed in a split second. We decided to go for it and went into the apartment. It looked and smelled exactly like my old home. Matter of fact I noticed that all old Soviet apartments look and smell the same. I could understand that they were all built by the same blueprint and yet my mind couldn't grasp how all of them could also smell exactly the same. It wasn't even a smell of a material or a food product, but a different one. Like many old people tend to smell similar after reaching a certain age. The same thing I noticed about apartments. The atmosphere that inhabited that apartment was old and tired, overstocked with items and drained by work and stress.

I took off my shoes and put my coat on a hanger and then, looked around once more trying to find Ian's mother. Upon looking into the kitchen. I saw an older woman sitting behind the table. She was drinking tea and was looking worried. I let her know of my presence, smiled and greeted her, though I didn't get a reaction. I didn't mind. I walked closer to her and sat at the other end of the table. She offered me tea. I thought about it for a second and accepted. I had some time and didn't want to seem impolite. She started to ask me where was her son and if everything was alright with him. I told her that he was alright, simply tired from working and wanted to go on a vacation. The decision was impulsive so he didn't have the time to warn everyone about his sudden departure. She calmed down. She indeed seemed to think that he did something to himself, so knowing that he was alive and we'll brought her a lot of closure. She smiled for once but that didn't indicate what I thought it did.

Then she started cussing me out as if I was her son. She had frustration in her I guess and wanted to let it out.

Once again, I didn't mind so I let her have it. By the time she was finishing, I started laughing out of nowhere because the whole situation seemed rather funny. She noticed that and laughed too. When we both recollected ourselves she apologised for the vile language, as I wasn't Ian and it was none of my fault. We laughed once again and as she was now calm I told her more about how we used to live together and how fun it was. She asked me if she could talk to him. I already had all of his new contacts, so I gave them to her. I set up all the connections and she sent him her first message. It looked like my job there was done and upon checking my phone there was also a message saying that my friends were waiting for me downstairs. I said my goodbyes and thanked them for their hospitality. They thanked me for coming through and before exiting I told them that if they needed anything or wanted to talk about something. They could call me at any time.

EVALUATING EXPERIENCES

Between rushing through the chaos and trying to figure out what to do next. I couldn't help it but watch Ian with utmost attention, as seemingly everything was orbiting around him at the time. The steady stream of news that kept bombarding us over the extent of those days affected us all. Ian was the one who happened to be in the heart of the storm, but to everyone's surprise he handled everything admirably well.

At first I myself had a hard time coping with what was going on. It was hard to wrap my mind around and somewhat scary to imagine, considering that I was the furthest from all the risks and drama. Ian on the contrary took everything rather peacefully and without any complaints or tantrums. He joked about it a little here and there, but mostly didn't make a big deal out of it. Looking back at it now. I find myself noticing that back then he didn't make a big deal out of anything that was going on around him. I'm not completely sure if he accepted everything with ease as he was waiting for something of that kind to happen. Or maybe he was simply calm on the surface, but deep inside he was going through a rollercoaster of emotions and thoughts. Maybe I will never know, maybe I will find out eventually. All I can say is that whatever I could see him reflect at the time was admirable. When the first news hit Ian was put face to face with a fact that he was about to say goodbye to the life he's been living so far. There was no other option, no other way out. He used all of his trump cards and was now facing prison time. All of his achievements, goals, relationships and comforts were about to vanish, as Ian was about to leave them all behind. If up until that very moment he was able to live comfortably and get by using the knowledge he already had and when in need, could always reach out to his friends and family. After the news dropped, he had to accept that those luxuries weren't available behind the borders of his hometown.

From time to time I've imagined myself in scenarios of such kind. Sometimes those thoughts came from curiosity, other times they came from fear. Both ways those scenarios weren't pleasant and nor did they create any uplifting emotions in me while I was imagining them. Whenever I caught myself being hanging in those imaginary scenarios. I snapped myself out of them and tried to dissolve them as quickly as possible. Noticing myself being caught up in those thought motivated me to be cautious. It reminded me that those scenarios were something I wanted to avoid, as they brought no good. When I realised that realities that I once imagined came to existence. Goosebumps ran across my back, making me feel a sensation of cold. I didn't really know how to react, what to do or what to say. All I could fathom was the fact that whatever was going on, wasn't happening directly to me. I was grateful, though it didn't change much as the situation was still very real and happening. Considering Ian's options and the mess he was in, by escaping the country as quickly as possible and not leaving any traces behind, he did us an enormous favour. His fast, selfless and brave actions granted us our relative freedom and comfort. The same freedom and comfort that allowed me to write this book in peace and quiet.

I watched how Ian took the news and what he did with the information that was given to him. Any person I know would panic, start crying or let their mind get consumed by chaotic images and fears. On the contrary Ian took everything with grace. Instead of letting his paranoid thoughts and emotions burst out into an incoherent storm, he took every word and piece of information as it was. No filters or selfish motives.

Only options in his consideration were the ones that were beneficial for the whole family. Instead of trying to save the comfortable reality that he was so used to and attempting to salvage whatever there was left of it. He understood that it was time for him to let go. The world that he was used to was no longer suitable for his growth. It no longer offered him anything which could contribute to his development.

Maybe Ian wasn't brave enough to let go of it on his own. Maybe he was too caught up in whatever he was doing to consider that whatever he was working on was no longer right for him. A million possible reasons could be listed for why he didn't do the step himself right away, but none of them would be right nor wrong. To be honest, no one is ever really ready for anything. I could be perfecting a piece of art or my own trait for as long as I live and never think that it's complete or perfect. I could be training for an eternity and still think that I'm not ready. Life will never wait for you to think that you're ready, because it considers you to be ready at all times and it really is so. The mind may think it's not good enough. In reality no one and everybody is ready at the same time and at all times. *You may never be completely prepared for anything, but you're always ready for everything that life may bring to your feet.* It's not about the circumstances or possessions, but the approach and mindset that is employed.

When Ian grasped the whole volume of the situation he was in. Many of his concerns and tasks he considered important simply fell off. They no longer held any relevancy or purpose as to function, they needed his constant attention and energy. With most of his activities now labelled as insufficient, he was left off with only a few things that were truly important to his heart. Ian's days in our country were counted. *The illusion of him having time fell apart in front if his eyes.* It didn't break him though, instead he got inspired. Every passing minute reminded him of what was truly important. Every time he noticed an hour pass, he remembered what was waiting for him. Possibly without his conscious will, the situation he was in forced him into being completely present in every moment he was in during those times. From the very second of his awakening, he submerged himself in whatever was going on in and outside of him. Feeling every passing second as if it was his first and last experience. Often our mind tends to make us think, that we have experienced something before or that the environment or situation we are in is familiar.

In reality everything constantly changes on many visible and invisible levels and really no experience is like the other. Every breakfast he cooked, was enjoyed in a completely different way. Ian tried to capture everything he could. Every emotion or sensation that became available to his senses. After snapping out of his daily dreams and activities, he fell in love with Kate in a completely new way. I tend to think that he became aware of the love she was giving him and became much more appreciative of it than ever before. He put aside everything that didn't truly make him happy and chose to spend his last days around his closest friends and family. Experiencing whatever he can and trying to feel as much love as he possibly could.

Watching Ian inspired me. It reminded me of where I was and why I was there, shifting my attention to my true motives. I looked at his approach and attitude. How calm and collected he was. How he managed to laugh and joke about his own seemingly unfortunate position. Ian wasn't miserable. He was alive. As much as I observed him. More I could see that I was surrounded with everything I ever wished for and even more. I became aware of my past goals and my goals at that time. I saw my girlfriend, dog and family in a completely new light. A wave of appreciation once again washed over me. It was blissful. I had everything. Whatever it was, it was being pulled apart and thrown across Europe, but it was still there. I understood that it was my purpose to spread love and maintain the wellbeing of the family that I was a part of. During those couple of days, Ian taught me a very valuable lesson. He taught me that the approach one employs in the given event, is what may play the crucial role in untangling that situation. Besides he also showed me how to appreciate things on a deeper level and that I shouldn't get carried away chasing daily businesses.

TOUGH LOVE

You're always ready for everything that life may bring to your feet. A sentence that made an appearance a couple pages earlier. I didn't include it on purpose, but when I was reading through the draft and saw it. It guided me to writing this chapter. Previously I've described humorous and somewhat sarcastic qualities of life or as I like to call it, the Universe. Mostly I've described my own experiences and how life has given me bitter lessons whenever I got comfortable or cocky. How only after struggles I became aware of those lessons being blessings in disguise and how much energy it took me to digest the new knowledge. In the end it took me some time to understand that I didn't have to struggle in order to grow. There have been quite many hints and references that got to shine throughout this book and all of them have been somewhat connected to this subject. Maybe previously they didn't make much sense or left an impression of verbal illustrations. Now I would like to describe the topic a bit more thoroughly and with more details.

Life doesn't make you face challenges you can't overcome. No matter how difficult or threatening the situation may seem to the mind, there's always a way out. You can get out of your problems just as easily as you got into them. The true questions are: *"Are you willing to put in the effort to find the solution?"* and *"Are you willing to bend your mind and habits enough, to be able to see and execute that solution?"* If both of those questions receive a positive answer. Any situation can find its solution. There's something very valuable I got to learn by observing my own mind. The mind likes to think that it knows everything. It's also lazy and prefers not to spend energy on solving problems and getting to results. It would much rather route that energy into worries and fears, thus without effort draining and exhausting you. It's okay though as it's not your fault. It's simply something it was conditioned and raised to do.

The origin of those beliefs and conditions is individual for everyone. Some were influenced more by the social media and the internet. Others were conditioned by the propaganda they were exposed to in newspapers or streets. You might be thinking *"Why is the mind like that?"* or *"Where does it come from?"* but neither of those questions have any importance.

Only question you should really consider is *"Am I willing to change?"* If you're willing to put in the effort in order to achieve a change. There's no challenge that you can't overcome.

Simply speaking. When you become aware of your goals and desires. Start to acknowledge that achieving those desires requires effort and stop making a big deal out of things that don't go your way. You'll be able to notice the flexibility of any moment and opportunity. You will no longer see misfortunate events as failures and will learn to easily find your way out of any situation. Of course you will first need to learn to accept everything as it is. When you're able to accept a situation as it is. Your surrounding can no longer control you and your emotions don't have the power to phase you. Though you are still there you can now see things without any distorted filters. That will allow you to free up some headspace and remember what your true goal was. With your desire in focus again and your energy not being thrown around aimlessly. You'll make it possible for yourself to find new solutions. Even If it won't work out right away or will take several attempts, the mindset that you have attained will now allow you to be flexible in any situation, instead of dwelling on fears and self-proclaimed failures.

A thought that once helped me to digest this whole concept went something like this. If you go back in time and look at some of the stressful situations, conflicts and moments you've had. You can clearly remember and even feel how stressful they were. You can feel how your heart rate increases and suddenly you get as anxious as if you were in that very moment again. You're not really there anymore but physically, emotionally and mentally you feel everything as if you were.

Then I remembered how those events got resolved. How after a while of stressing, I figured out that there was no practical use in doing that. I focused on finding a solution and as if by help of an invisible hand everything got resolved. After that those stressful situations no longer looked so scary or impossible. Then another thought cut off the previous one. If I've gone through so many stressful situations, stressed while I was in there and later figured that all that stressing was unnecessary. Then why do I start stressing as soon as a seemingly stressful situation comes up? It's not like I evaluated everything and then started worrying. It became clear to me that stressing was a habit or a triggered action that happened subconsciously. With that thought in mind, I slowly started to understand that if I didn't give in to that pattern of stressing and worrying right away. If I skipped it and focused on looking for the solution. I could potentially save a lot of energy and direct it in better areas. I wouldn't hurt myself with abusive thoughts and emotional pain. I didn't need any more reasons to try. When that understanding started to sink in my being. I started to see how many situations no longer irritated or stressed me. I started to feel more energised and calm. Whatever I approached got done much quicker and with no struggles whatsoever. Situations were still challenging but I no longer felt attacked by them. After some time, that type of thinking became habitual and going through life became much easier. I managed to notice and let go of an abusive habit and it felt amazing.

The topics and subjects I've been describing along the main story, may seem strange or confusing at first however, it's okay as they're here for a reason. In the end of this book I'll try to form these subjects into practical exercises that you'll be able to try out for yourself and know if you find them useful or not.

HOLDING ON TO PROMISES

Ian's absence didn't affect our work too heavily. The fact that he was away simply made us go to work a little earlier as we had to complete his tasks alongside ours. In a few days it already became a norm. Soon I and David started to see that our business system needed improvements once again. Doing Ian's job alongside ours required more energy and attention. As it was now just the two of us, we figured that it would be smarter to rearrange tasks and possibly hire someone to work for us. We decided to focus on improving our business and maintaining the wellbeing of our little family. While handing work, we occasionally went out and hosted some family activities. From time to time we messaged Ian to know how he was doing and if he needed any money. He was doing well though. He was quickly adopting to his new habitat and was in the process of learning the local language. He had a place where to live and was also looking for a job to support himself better. When I heard those things I felt proud and happy for him.

It didn't take us long before we found a person to hire and our work became easier once more. Hiring an employee turned out to be a great investment. It saved us a lot of time and energy and though it cost us a bit, the growth in our profits covered that quickly. Things at home were decent too. My girl was pursuing her dream and was quickly growing her customer base and was already being recognised by experienced local artists. Kate was becoming happier and happier. I don't know what really prompted it but I was glad to observe the process. She didn't look depressed anymore. Her skin was no longer pale and the spark in her eyes became visible again. She started to engage in conversations much more often. If in the past she didn't speak much and nor could she speak English very well then now she was learning quickly and spoke with confidence.

It felt like everything was slowly getting better. Step by step, one day at a time I could see how our situation was improving.

One morning I was in the kitchen watching something on the internet while eating my second breakfast, when Kate ran out of her room half naked with a lit cigarette in her hand. Her eyes were on fire and she couldn't stand still even for a second. In her broken yet uplifted and confident English she said: *"Guys. You know. In two weeks, I move to Ian. We live together now."* Slightly but pleasantly surprised. All I could say was: *"Cool! Did he find a place for both of you?"* To which she replied with a joyful *"Yes."* It turned out that Ian really found a place and a way to bring his girlfriend along and support her. I was happy for Kate. She's been waiting and wishing for it and now it was about to happen. Two weeks and a couple thousand kilometres were separating Kate from Ian. It was no longer uncertain. Ian did what he had promised and Kate was about to be next to him.

The next two weeks were eventful but on a major scale. Nothing serious happened. We didn't get bamboozled and no problems occurred at work either. No frightening news came in and so we got to enjoy a bit of peace. As we knew that Kate was leaving soon and we were already missing Ian. We wanted to spend more time with her doing something together. We watched a lot of movies and cooked meals side by side. Went on walks with our dog and simply chatted as much as we could. She often told us that as soon as she arrived we were expected to visit them. I laughed and told her that we were indeed going to see them. We didn't know when yet but that was going to become clear in the near future. Kate was truly excited to go. She told her whole family about her upcoming departure and though it was a surprise to everyone, nobody got really worried. Kate knew what she was doing and she knew that Ian was going to take care of her well.

The time we spent with Kate was great, so we wanted to embrace it to the fullest. When those two weeks exceeded. We drove Kate to the airport to spend the last two hours with her. We laughed and talked about our mutual memories and things we did while we lived together. We remembered every funny situation that happened at home and laughed about the things we were going to do upon our visit. The two hours we had with her passed quickly. Kate and her best friend shared a long hug and cried for a minute until it was time for Kate to head to the gates. We said our goodbyes and even though Kate was still right there, I could already feel her absence sinking in. I acknowledged the bitter sensation I got in my stomach but brushed it off. It was life after all. Things like that happen all the time. Upon returning home I could feel the change in the atmosphere before I even opened the front door. It was similar to the change that happened when Ian left, though now it was even more present. It was quieter, emptier and somewhat colder. The cozy little home was no longer as cozy as it used to be.

CONCLUSIONS:
KNOWING WHEN TO STOP

It was late November. The temperature was decreasing steadily and days turned notably shorter. During day time the sky was mostly cloudy. The sun could barely shine through and only on occasional nights one could see the stars shining. Some time had passed since Kate left and the remaining members of our family slowly started to get used to the new atmosphere. Though the heating system in our floors worked on full steam at all times, it still couldn't warm our house the same way our cozy little family once did.

Though days and months long lost their meanings in my eyes. I acknowledged that another busy week was coming to an end. For the past year I've been living like every day was a Saturday. Nevertheless I still appreciated weekends, on those days no business was conducted and therefore I could relax more thoroughly. That Sunday morning I woke up early, the sun was shining right into the window of my bedroom. I felt rested and had energy. Though the thought process wasn't active yet, something deep within me knew that day was special. I stood up and got myself dressed. My dog was already awake and wagging her tail, excited to experience the upcoming day. We went downstairs. While I cooked breakfast, I fed the dog and got her prepared for her annual morning walk. After clothing myself, I attached the leash to her collar and we went outside. The sky was clear and I could see no clouds. I could feel the sun warm my skin, making the cold wind more or less bearable. We walked around for a couple minutes as she got to do her business after which we went

back upstairs. The family was still asleep. There was no need to wake them up either so I decided to quietly watch something on the internet while I planned the upcoming week. While I was watching some insignificant video, I remembered my parents and the fact that I hadn't seen them for a while.
I knew they were home, it was Sunday after all. I looked over my tasks and schedule. There was nothing urgent or important. The decision was almost made. I picked up my phone and called dad. The phone rang a couple times and he picked up. It took him about a minute until he walked outside the house and I could finally understand his speech. Though my parents built themselves a pretty modern house. They decided to place it in the middle of thick woods with barely any signal. They didn't even have any neighbours in their surrounding so you could say that they were living a rather private lifestyle. I told him I was having a free day and could come over. His voice got excited and he offered to pick me up in about two hours. I agreed and our call ended there. I began packing my bag and a couple things for the dog. I wanted to take her with me to let her run around the woods. After packing my notebooks, pens and other utilities in the backpack. I told my girlfriend that I was leaving for the day and started getting dressed. Dad called soon after, telling me to come downstairs. I called for my dog, leashed her and we went out.

While we were driving towards my parent's house, we passed all the locations I grew up seeing. Roads I used to walk on foot and houses I passed on a bicycle. Fields me and my friends crossed and forests that I've walked during many winters. As we entered the woods, I could already feel the relief. The trees that surrounded me made me feel safe and calm. I grew up in those woods, I knew every corner and every edible plant that was there. That place felt like home. When we reached their house and got out of the car. I could instantly feel how all the worries and thoughts that I brought with me from the city started to fall off and lose their importance. A heavy rock fell from my chest and I could breathe again. The air was cold and scratched my throat. Sun was no longer as high and not as warming as in the morning. I unleashed the dog and she ran off in a pursuit of joy. I walked around the yard for a little, reminiscing the childhood memories I could recollect.

All sorts of memories came up. I remembered how as a six years old I used to play at the construction of that house.

The building process just started and only the foundation was there. It was around December. I and my mom were playing in the snow. Looking back at it made me feel warm on the inside. All the emotions I felt that moment returned and filled my body. I was happy. Then I remembered how on the very spot I was standing on, over a year ago my first conscious journey started. A sensation arose in my stomach. I didn't know what it was or how to react to it. It was something completely new to me. The sensation came from my own body, meaning that it wasn't alien to me. On the other hand possibly it was the first time I noticed it. Then again I didn't know what to do with it and soon I lost the sensation. It's been some time since I arrived and I started to feel cold. The sun was already on its way down and I decided it was time for us to go inside. When I entered through the heavy metal front door a familiar smell entered my nostrils. Another wave of warm emotions hit me. Even though I couldn't call that house my home, it was still a place where I felt peaceful and safe. As I was taking off my shoes, my dog already ran into the kitchen, from where I later heard my mom's voice. I followed her voice and as I saw her, we greeted each other and shared a hug. She told me that my brother was home too and that I should go and say hello to him as well. I was in a great mood so I did just as she said. When I returned downstairs, I sat by the fire that was in the middle of their living room. Warmth that came from the fireplace hit my body, pleasantly warming it up after an extended walk. I sat there for a while. The city exhausted me. I was jumpy, tired and confused to an extent. I was in a desperate need for a pause. I needed some time to calm down, rearrange my thoughts and priorities to see. What was my position and where I was heading.

After some time I was still sitting on a couch in front of the fireplace. My body was no longer cold and the weight of the social life which followed me from the city was now finally dissolving. My mind was slowly clearing up and most of my senses got to rest as the house was quiet and soundproof. Occasional footsteps and crackling of burning wood were the only things that were audibly present. A thought emerged in my mind. It was of somebody telling me that I should turn to my mother more often. The thought reminded me that my mom was still doing something in the kitchen. There was also nothing better to do so I decided to follow the thought and see what it could possibly bring. I stood up and walked a couple steps until I was in the kitchen. I cleared my throat to notify her of my presence. I wasn't too sure if she noticed me walking in and as I didn't want to scare her I chose the safe route. She turned around and looked at me. I told her that I was slightly confused and needed some answers. We sat down behind their kitchen table as she implied and started our discussion. She asked me if something was wrong and I told her that there wasn't. Everything was good. I simply needed some guidance. I expressed my concerns about not knowing what goals to pursue or what to do next. Seemingly I had achieved everything I wanted. What was left to accomplish was in the process and I had no doubt that those things will be manifesting soon enough. *"Well. If there's nothing that's really bothering you, why don't you just go upstairs and meditate? Maybe the answers will come to you themselves."* There was still some time until I could go to the sauna and nothing much else to do, so I decided to do as she said. I felt slightly better. Not because she told me something new or something I didn't notice before, but simply because I talked to her. Though I and my mother are very similar, we don't talk much. The feeling of peace that emerged in my stomach from simply opening up to her was great. I thanked her for her time and got up. I called for my dog and as soon as she was next to me, we went upstairs.

When my mom told me to go upstairs and meditate, she meant a certain place. In my parent's house everything had a designated location. As a child, whenever I used something and left it laying around. Mom always got pissed off because of it and lectured me on being careless. As expected there was a certain room for meditations. It was my old room which was rebuilt into a half wardrobe half meditation room. The space where my bed used to stand was turned into a big cabinet for clothes. The remainder of the room was empty except an imported Indian carpet. I sat down on the carpet and crossed my legs. My dog walked around for about a minute and sat next to me. I closed my eyes and started meditating. The thought process in my head stopped. The voice that once narrated my days and commented on everything got silent. There were no pictures in my mind's eye and I fell into complete and utter silence. I could feel my blood flow and my heart beat. I was aware of my whole body and could feel different parts of my body I usually didn't notice. It was fun but not the reason I was there. I pointed my awareness at my current being and my desired being. Though no clear answer came to me, the relaxation and clarity that followed were very pleasant. After about an hour of meditating, I opened my eyes and my awareness returned to the present space. I looked at the clock, time indicated that the sauna was ready. I shook off the slight haze in which I was after that meditation and left the room to get a towel.

When I opened the glass door that separated the sauna from the shower room, I almost coughed from the heat entering my lungs. The sauna was indeed hot and ready. I sat on the highest shelf and crossed my legs. Being in the sauna always gave me a sensation of purification. As if sweating detoxed my physical body and enduring heat cleansed my mind from any unimportant thoughts. I sat there for a while meditating with my eyes open. I didn't want to close them, because passing out in a hot closed space wasn't something I was going for on a relaxed Sunday. Plus meditating with eyes open is just as good as doing so with closed eyes.

After about three rounds, I decided it was time to go outside and cool off a little. It was already dark outside. The only source of light that was around and illuminated the surface was the moon that was unusually luminous and big that night. I walked out of the sauna and saw my body steaming. It wasn't anything special, but it did humour me. I walked around the yard barefoot for a while, feeling the grass beneath me. It was cold and wet, I could feel the frozen needles stabbing my soles. It reminded me of my first journey. As that thought was floating around my mind, I became aware of my current surrounding and circumstances and looked up in the sky. It was clear. There were no clouds and clusters of stars that could be seen clearly. I froze. All of a sudden all thoughts got sucked out of my mind and I couldn't take my eyes off the stars. They looked exactly like that night, but this time I was completely sober. The most memorable events flashed in front of my eyes in a split second and a sudden understanding came over me. I was no longer confused. I knew that everything that happened came into existence for a reason. All of those events taught me valuable lessons and without me even noticing it, guided me along the desires I wished for. I had everything I asked for. I felt blessed. I was happy and grateful for being alive and felt that my happiness came from simply being alive. It wasn't about material possessions or my status. I was happy because every morning I could wake up and experience. If before I was confused and wasn't completely sure if I knew where I was supposed to go after accomplishing my goals. After looking at the stars that night, I knew. I didn't know exactly where to go, who to talk to or where to get something that would aid me along my path, but I knew what I was supposed to do, to figure all those things. I had to stop. It was time for me to stop and look at my progress. Did I do everything the way I wanted to? Did I learn all the lessons I was supposed to? Does everything feel harmonious or is there something that could be better?

I started to feel cold again, so I went back inside. After another round in the sauna, I took a shower, got myself dressed and went back to my parent's house. I thanked them for their hospitality and the advice they gave me and went back home. I was happy and I felt relieved. I was glad I was going home with some answers and some ideas on what I should do next.

The understanding that I was now holding in me was like a clarification and a confirmation. It told me I was on the right path and that besides some minor adjustments I should keep moving forward. When I got home I unleashed the dog once again and gave her some food. When activities of such kind were completed I got out my papers and started working on myself. As I said, I didn't know exactly what to do or where to look, but I knew what to do in order to figure out the direction in which I was supposed to look. I wrote down all of my past goals, the ones I achieved and the ones I didn't accomplish yet. I wrote down my current progress and the new goals that were born along the way. I deconstructed them and thought about things that were required for success. Soon enough my rough drafts started to look more coordinated and eventually formed a plan. After looking at it, it became clear to me that everything was fine. I regained some mental clarity and my heart felt more at peace. The daily hustle I was going through, together with all the meetings, e-mails, business ventures, family things and all, took a lot of my energy and attention. As I was caught up in those things, I couldn't see the bigger picture and remember, that all those things were contributing to my goals. It felt good. I put away my papers and went to sleep happy.

STOP

I don't want to sound like an annoying parent, but I do want to stress the importance of knowing when to stop. I'm not saying that after reaching some point or after some time you should stop and completely cut off the given activity. No. That would be a nonsense. What I'm saying is much more simple and logical than the radical example above.

Every now and then, it's good to stop and look around. It's healthy to take small breaks. Pauses allow you to rest and they take your attention away from all the action, therefore allowing you to see the bigger picture. Of course you can do all those things while being about that business but when all your energy and attention is being routed somewhere, you can't reflect as practically. Putting all your important tasks and mundane routines away for a moment and relaxing is a great thing to do from time to time. You can regain your energy and look around without stressing. While being on that kind of a break, I recommend evaluating your activities and goals. Did you make any progress? Did you achieve any goals? Did your activities develop you on your path? Are your goals and desires still relevant or did they change along the way? Maybe you could do something better? Could there be a more practical way to do something? Could you achieve your next goal more conveniently?

Stopping every once in a while and asking the same questions all over again may sound ridiculous at first, but as the world moves in cycles it's really nothing out of the ordinary. It's a simple practice that can help you release some stress, free your headspace and attain a certain knowing if what you're doing is right for you or not. In the best case, you receive a confirmation that you're doing well and should carry on moving forward. In the worst case so to say, you would simply understand that you need so change something or look in another direction.

THE INTERNAL SPRING

A couple peaceful days passed. I took some time off to reflect and relax. Many things had happened during the past year and there were a ton of things on my mind that needed answers or at least some type of clarifications. After feeling as if I emptied a trash big into my own head, it felt good to finally have clarity and peace dominating in my being.

By the end of those days, I had multiple sheets of paper mapping my mind, desires, goals and issues I wanted to resolve. Not to be mistaken, those so called maps didn't look anything like geographic maps nor did they look like a solid plan. They had many unknowns and variables, meaning that there was a lot of space for improvisation and different opportunities. Learning from my past mistakes and lessons, I didn't want my mind to have expectations or a solid plan that it would follow. I simply wanted to cut off all the unnecessary thoughts that in no way contributed to my growth or the process of achieving my goals.

The rest was simply remembering my true goals and following my heart without any doubts. All the trash that was piled up in my head was now disposed. I knew exactly what I wanted and how I wanted it. Desires that weren't completely clear were developing on the way, so neither there was a need to stress over not knowing those. I was rested and could feel how energy was flowing through my being. My mind was at peace and I heard no parasitic chatter in my head. The decisions I made came from my heart and were true to me, making the actions I later conducted precise and fruitful results.

As if intended by the Universe, things started working out just right. I and my friend Hakan started working together again. If in the past our business ventured weren't very successful, then now they were more profitable than ever before. We started collaborating more closely and soon enough he introduced me to his another friend Goggy. An older Georgian man, a lawyer by education and a hustler by nature. A man I never truly learnt to understand, but quickly grew accustomed to and accepted in my close circle of friends and family. Working with Hakan and Goggy was exciting and challenging at the same time. We were all from different cultural backgrounds, meaning that the ways we spoke the same language were different. Though the words we spoke sounded the same, often they meant very different things. Nevertheless that didn't stop us from getting that bread together, as we managed to have a lot of fun on the way. It looked like everything was getting better again. There were no conflicts or problems. The improvements we got to implements thanks to Hakan's Eastern connections and Goggy's speaking talent made our business run much smoother, meaning that we had to spend less time attending it. Aside from work, I finally felt like I had written enough material and was now ready to start writing my first book. I knew that it was going to take some time. There were many drafts I had to review and then rewrite. I wanted to make sure everything I wrote was interesting and somewhat valuable, so I excluded the thought of rushing the project. It felt good to be back doing something I truly enjoyed. I found infinite joy and pleasure in writing that book and every action or situation that was a part of that process. From time to time I exchanged messages with Ian and Kate. Hearing from them was always pleasant and heartwarming. Especially when they told me that they were happy and that for them too everything was working out perfectly.

It looked like after all the stress and hustle we finally reached a point where we could relax for a moment and figure what we wanted to do next. There were no Arturs to drain our money or Azeri mob chasing our friends or offering us their services. No maniacs or psychopaths from Poland and no threats or news from the government. My heart felt at ease and I could really focus on things that were truly important to me. My family and sharing my experiences, in order to help others be more productive in whatever field they choose.

First snow came down in the middle of November and it was now cold and windy every day. Ian and Kate were doing great and invited us to visit them for the New Year's celebration. We accepted it without thinking and started planning our trip. Work was going just as it was supposed to and didn't need to be overlooked as much as before. Though I felt unconditionally happy and blissful from simply being alive. I still knew that there were many challenges before me and that I still had to learn countless lessons until I would achieve everything my heart desires.

PRACTICAL EXERCISES & MEDITATIONS

To make the whole story more illustrative and easy to read. I excluded many paragraphs, events, lessons and observations so I wouldn't deviate from the main course. After reading the manuscript it felt like something was missing. I didn't just want to share my story. It wasn't that outstanding and besides, every person alive is living their own exciting story. Why would they care for mine? My primary desire was to share something that would aid others in achieving their goals and desires. Something that would make their road to victory smoother. I'm not saying that it would make it less rocky, but it could potentially widen their awareness, so they could go around those rocks better or fix their tires quicker without losing courage or motivation.

The first time I stumbled on these practices was when I myself was going through difficulties. Discovering these exercises taught me discipline and expanded my awareness. They helped me to calm down and figure out where to look for answers or solutions. Through these meditations I found out how to listen to my internal signals more attentively and how to recognise my intuition or the best time for action. The desire to share practices I discovered through experience first came to me when my close friend Yaz asked me for advice. The answer that helped her emerged from the experience I went through and deconstructed a while ago. From then on, I paid more attention to my experiences and methods I practiced during those exercises. It turned out that when applied properly, they turned out to be quite potent. Helping people around me has always been a subtle passion of mine. Since then I found a way how I could do it even better. I also knew that I couldn't help someone who didn't want to be aided and that it wasn't always good to intervene with people's karma. In order to save myself from unnecessary situations, I developed a personal rule.

"Don't give people advice you wouldn't give to your kids." Meaning that I wouldn't give an advice I wouldn't consider helpful for my child. Having someone's trust has always been a kind of a responsibility. I didn't want to be responsible for a person getting hurt or being misled.

Then again, whatever I'm about to share is completely useless in theory or without actual application. What's the use of having a driver's license if there's no car available? What's the point of a lamp if it's never turned on? I would say that the upcoming content is useful only when there's purpose for using it. It has value when you know exactly what you're using it for. It's most potent when you're using it with awareness, knowing exactly how you're using it and for what result you're putting it into application.

Deconstructing as a Practice

* Pick a subject or a situation you wish to deconstruct.

* Write down and describe everything that is causing you discomfort. Write down where and how it's affecting you in an unpleasant way. Don't forget to describe, why does that thing bother you in the first place?

* Into another column, write down your desired state of being. What is that you desire? Describe your perfect world in detail. When those things are written. Write down the reasons that are holding you back from experiencing that perfect being or achieving the desired reality?

* You should be seeing your problem or situation with two columns under it. One describing the roots of your situation and the second one describing the desired solution.

* Now you should be aware of your problem (if it can be called such), what needs to be changed, what needs to be achieved and how it will be enjoyed. It's about time to start figuring out how you're going to get to those desired results.

* You can start off by writing down things you'd need to change about yourself or your approach, in order to achieve those results. You can look at it as if it's a puzzle you're trying to complete. What actions could be conducted more practically? Are there any options you haven't tried? Have you been looking in the right direction or there are opportunities around you that you haven't noticed yet? Have you been following a pattern? Does that pattern need a change?

* Now that you've deconstructed the situation to an extent. You've got a clearer overview of your situation. What you desire and what you wish to let go of. What you have already tried and what is yet to be tried. What you have now can be used as a reminder or a map in your daily life, so you wouldn't get confused or disoriented again and would be able to reach those desired results more swiftly.

Mapping Desires

* Take a piece of paper and divide it into three columns. Middle column being *Soul Desires*, left being *Mind Desires* and right being *Physical Desires*.

* Start with *Physical Desires*. Write down all the physical possessions and qualities you wish to have. Cars, houses, pets, clothes, money etc. Everything you believe would aid you on your path of life. How would those possessions help you in achieving your *Mind Desires* and *Soul Desires*?

* Continue to *Mind Desires*. Describe what mental qualities and possessions could aid you in achieving those *Physical Desires* and *Soul Desires*?

* Lastly look deep into your heart. Try to distance yourself from your ego and try letting your heart or soul speak. Write down what you feel is your purpose for being alive. What achievements, actions or ways of being make you truly happy? What is that drives you on daily basis?

* Now it's time to think. How well you're pursuing your *Soul Desires*. Are those desires true to you or have they been influenced? Are the *Mind Desires* helping along in achieving your Soul Desires or are they conflicting? Are your *Physical Desires* doing the same or are they more of an abusive nature?

* When you have thought about all those things. It would be necessary to erase the desires that don't feel true to you or are conflicting with your *Soul Desires*. Cut off everything that doesn't feel natural or doesn't contribute to your happiness. It's important to be honest with oneself. If honesty with self is avoided, this practice will bring nothing but further confusion.

* When the list you've made feels natural and true to you. Start figuring how you can use that list for achieving the desires written on it and how to do it more practically and with less stress and hustle.

Relocating the Self

* Relocating the Self is easiest when done in a form of a mind map. Make a circle in the middle of a paper and write *"Present"* in it. Under that circle, make a second one and write *"In Progress"* in it. On the right, make another circle with *"Future"* and another circle under it with *"Close Future"* in it. On the left, make a circle with *"Completed"* and another one with *"False"* written within.

* Start by writing down everything you desire to have and to be in the future and connect those points to the *"Future"* circle.

* Then write down your short term goals and things that you believe could contribute to getting to them. Hopefully those short term goals can also aid you in accomplishing your long term goals. After writing them down, connect them to the *"Close Future"* circle.

* Now to see your relative progress and further encourage yourself. Write down all the goals you have completed. From minor successes to grand achievements. Write down as much as you can and see, how well you have done and how much potential you're holding within.

* It's time to look at what you have. What is it telling you? Are you seeing any goals that are no longer relevant to you? Are you seeing anything that's not quite true for you? Anything that doesn't resonate with you like it used to?

* Things that no longer make you feel inspired or no longer drive you can be written down under the *"False"* circle. Write them down to see, what is no longer relevant and let go of it. Writing those things down simply helps you to let go quicker and more efficiently.

* Now that you know where you're standing, how much you've done and what is yet to be done. You can see what you can start handing right away and what goals need some work. It's about time you start putting your plans and intentions to work.

Reflecting

* Take a look at events in your life that left a mark on you. Look at them without attachment or identification. What lessons did they teach you? To what did they open your eyes to?

* List your achievements. What did they teach you? How can you apply the knowledge received from them now? What benefits do these achievements give you?

* Look at the life you've lived so far from your new point of view. From your most recent and least attached perspective. What have you learnt? How much valuable experience have you collected? Acknowledge all the material you have in your possession that you can apply at any given moment.

* Now look at your past and see how it has improved some aspects of your life that led you to your current position. See how much good all those seemingly inconvenient situations caused. Find mercy within and forgive yourself for reacting negatively or blaming somebody else for whatever. Forgive yourself, everybody else and the world your living in included. Everything that has happened, has granted you valuable experience that you can use at any time to better your life in your desired direction.

* Think how you can use that experience now and tomorrow to improve your current situation and start steering your ship in your truly desired direction.

* Start thinking how through now you can start bringing your future into the present moment. Making it no longer future, but the blissful and eternal now. Think how you could turn your current unfulfilled reality into the desired happy reality. You don't have to chase the future when you can apply all the desired qualities to your present moment.

Awareness

* Become aware of your goal. Understand the purpose of your current and upcoming actions. Remember the reasons for your precious acts.

* Become aware of what needs to be changed and why it needs to be changed.

* Open yourself up to new possibilities that can aid you in achieving your desired changes. Open your awareness and see how the opportunities start revealing themselves. Be ready to step into action and utilise those opportunities for your purposes.

* Become aware of your senses and how they're reacting to your thoughts and emotions. Become aware how your goals and desires affect your senses.

* Become aware of your surrounding and how it's reacting to your thoughts, desires and actions. Is it helping you along or is it trying to warn you?

* Observe, deconstruct and adopt. Look around and within. Become aware of your progress and see if you're moving in your desired direction. What changed in and around you? Do you need to further change something or maybe you need to readopt to your current surrounding or find a way to get used to your new one?

AN INSIGHT INTO THE FUTURE

Before I finish this book, there are a few more things I would like to share. While I was collecting experiences and materials for this book, I understood that there are many more things I would like to share than subjects I could fit into this story. During those one and a half years I encountered many interesting observations and stumbled upon many practices that aided me not only in my personal growth and awareness, but in knowing how to interact with society and nature as well. Why I couldn't include everything I wanted in this one book, is simply because the contents of it would be too sporadic and incoherent to sound credible. It would be too difficult to read in the end, I just didn't want to waste my or any other individual's time.

Nevertheless I do hope every individual that decided to read this book found it interesting and engaging. Maybe even found something useful for their lives. Though as I can't know for certain how this piece will be received or if it will find its way to the bigger audience at all. I won't say too much or give any promises. All I can say is that if I see people being interested in this book and become aware of the fact that content of such kind is in demand. I will be glad to share my other observations which I got to experience and interpret into practical texts for better being in society, nature and life in general. If this piece of work finds its way to the public, we can consider it to be the introduction to a series of books.

A series about personal development and wider awareness. About nature and how we can interact with it better and live more harmoniously. About our society and how to grow in it more conveniently.

I'm happy this book made its way from my imagination to reality. I'm grateful for every experience that led me to writing it and every person who became a part of it. I appreciate every lesson that this life has taught me and for everything that is yet to come. Thank you. Thank you. Thank you.

REFERENCES, INSPIRATIONS & SOURCES

"The Alchemist" by Paulo Coelho
"The 7 Spiritual Laws of Success" by Deepak Chopra
"The Tibetan Book of Living & Dying" by Sogyal Rinpoche
"The Three Questions" by Don Miguel Ruiz
"The Art of Dreaming" by Carlos Castaneda
"The Path of a Shaman" by Michael Harner
"Becoming Supernatural" by Dr. Joe Dispenza
"The Wisdom of the Shamans" by Don Jose Ruiz
"The Deeper Wound: Recovering the Soul" by Deepak Chopra
"A New Earth: Awakening to your Life's Purpose"
by Eckhart Tolle
"The Power of Now: A Guide to Spiritual Enlightenment"
by Eckhart Tolle
"The Power of Silence" by Carlos Castaneda